THE

THEORY

OF

THE COMMON LAW.

BY

JAMES M. WALKER,

CHARLESTON, S. C.

"At jus privatum sub tutela juris publici."—BACON.

THE LAWBOOK EXCHANGE, LTD.

UNION, NEW JERSEY

1998

ISBN 1-886363-45-5

Printed in the United States of America
On Acid-Free Paper

Please see catalogue at rear of this book
for other titles reprinted by:

The Lawbook Exchange, Ltd.
965 Jefferson Avenue
Union, New Jersey 07083-8605

http://www.lawbookexc.com

Library of Congress Cataloging-in-Publication Data

Walker, James M. (James Murdock), 1813-1854.
The theory of the common law / by James M. Walker.
p. cm.
Originally published : Boston : Little, Brown and Co., 1852.
Includes bibliographical references.
ISBN 1-886363-45-5 (cloth : alk. paper)
1. Common law—Great Britain—History. 2. Common law—Roman influences. I. Title.
KD671.W34 1998
340.5'7—dc21 98-9522
CIP

THEORY

OF

THE COMMON LAW.

THE THEORY OF THE COMMON LAW.

BY

JAMES M. WALKER,
CHARLESTON, S. C.

"At jus privatum sub tutela juris publici." — BACON.

BOSTON:
LITTLE, BROWN AND COMPANY.
1852.

CAMBRIDGE:
METCALF AND COMPANY,
PRINTERS TO THE UNIVERSITY.

TO

THE HON. MITCHELL KING,

CHARLESTON, S. C.

SIR:—

Permit me, under your auspices, to deliver to the profession the following tractate on the law. Its object is to exhibit the leading thought of that noble system of jurisprudence, the Common Law, which you cultivated with so great success during your attendance on the bar. The reference which I make frequently to the Civil Law will not, I trust, be distasteful to one who is so conversant with Roman literature. No one is better qualified than yourself, both in regard to a knowledge of the Common Law and the Civil, to estimate the value and difficulty of my task, or to give to the attempt a more indulgent consideration. Moreover, be pleased to accept this dedication as a tribute of the respect and regard of "an apprentice to the law" to his former master.

Your obedient servant,

JAMES M. WALKER.

CONTENTS.

INTRODUCTION.

PART I.

The science of law, in its most comprehensive sense, is the body of rules of human conduct which are universally recognized as obligatory. In a more limited view, it is the body of rules which constitute the code of a particular state. But in either sense, the basis of every system must be truth. The universal is true, because it is consistent with the nature of man; the municipal is true, because it is consistent with the nature of the people subject to it. The truth of the municipal is not, however, the antagonist of the truth of the universal. For a law of a particular state may also be a law of humanity, or it may, as the law of aliens, be the law of every nation, without being the law of nature. The municipal differs from the universal only as a particular differs from a general truth.

A body of laws implies necessarily internal concordance or harmony of its rules. This agreement renders the multitude of special rules a law, a unity. They are together one law; thus we say, the law of England, the law of nations, the law of nature. A law signifies the relation of man to man; a body of laws, the relation of nation to nation; the universal law, the relation of man to God. When a law has been adopted by a people from the universal, then that law, the relation of man to man, is the true relation between man and man in the municipal and universal, — is a special and general truth. That which is the true relation between man and man is the just relation, or justice, — absolute as to the universal, relative as to the municipal. So, also, a law expresses not only the relation of man to man, but at the same time his relation to the supreme power. In like manner, a body of laws, the law of England, taken as a unit, must have to the law of every other nation and to the supreme power the relation of the true and just; else those living according to that law will be enemies of mankind and the supreme power that governs them.

As the law of each nation differs in important respects from that of every other, each unit is different in its nature, its tendency, and its mode of expression. Now, to constitute a unit of a multitude of rules, there must be some one idea which has affinity to every rule, and around which all may harmoniously be grouped. That idea will control the law in every part, and in all its modes of expression. It will determine the tendency of each system, and stamp upon it its own peculiar characteristics. That idea is the life of the law, and animates every member of the body politic. It begins with the birth, lives in the history, and dies in the last scene of the national drama. It must be found in every relation of man to man and to society. The men of high and the men of low degree, each family and each child, all property, history, and literature, must bear its indelible impression. That idea is, in short, the eminent truth of that people; an exposition of it in its application to law is the philosophy of law.

The philosophical element of the law must be equally applicable to the public and private law of a state; else there would not be the law, but the laws, of England. In other words, one people would be subject to two coequal and discordant systems. The truth being then the same in both branches, the public and the private, its discovery in one is conclusive of its existence in the other branch. Our inquiry leads us to consider whether there exists in the Common Law an idea with the consequences which we have specified. How does that idea express itself in that system? What are its effects upon the people, its influence upon other systems, its power in directing the movements of the mind of humanity. These questions are within the province of the philosophical statesman. Our task is the humble one of establishing the existence of such an idea in the Common Law, and exhibiting its control over the rules of property peculiar to that system.

An indispensable instrument in the investigation of all scientific truth is method. Science cannot exist without it. Now our juridical writers altogether neglect it. For although the law is a collection of principles, they treat of it, not in reference to principles, — the abstract, — but in reference to things, — the concrete. They neither descend from general to particular, the ordinary mode of imparting scientific information, nor ascend from particulars to generals, the ordinary method of discovering truth. This is the more remarkable, inasmuch as the science of the law has been not inaptly termed one of the exact sciences. The geometric or demonstrative method has been applied with remarkable success to the solution of questions of law. And that it deserves to rank as a science almost in the same class with geometry can easily be made apparent. Its terms are free from ambiguity, its first principles simple and obvious, the subjects with which it is conversant are wholly independent of things in actual visible existence, and are capable of being accurately defined. Their properties and relations are immutable. In these respects both sciences have the same qualities. Our surprise is not lessened by the consideration, that, whilst other moral sciences have been discussed in every variety of method, it should have been altogether neglected in a science which of all others is the most intimately acquainted with human relations, — by which man lives, moves, and has his being in society, — which makes his home a temple and a fortress, that no impious hand can touch with impunity, no daring adversary assail with success. But its neglect is a fact now, and was when Bacon pronounced this judgment upon his age: "Qui de legibus scripserunt omnes, vel tanquam philosophi, vel tanquam jurisconsulti argumentum illud tractaverunt. Atque philosophi proponunt multa dictu pulchra, sed ab usu remota. Jurisconsulti autem ..... placitis obnoxii et addicti ..... tanquam e vinculis sermocinantur."

It is in this respect that the Roman has so great advantage over the Common Law. The universal error of our juridical writers is in supposing that, even in those countries over which the Civil Law presides, it is valued chiefly for its doctrines. The reverse is the truth. "When," says Professor Mayer, on the subject of the use of the Civil Law in Germany, "its provisions shall have ceased to have the force of law, its study will produce greater profit, and the peculiar method employed by the so-called jurists in treating the law will be better estimated and turned to practical account." Again he says, "It ought ever to be remembered, that, familiar as they (the Roman lawyers) were with all the culture of their times, they knew the law not as an aggregate of rules, but in its scientific unity, such as it was disclosed to them by its own history and the history of their nation. The legal literature of no other people can show a casuistry so thoroughly spiritual, where the matter of fact only seems designed to corporealize and exhibit the spirit. Hence, there is no better training of practitioners than the study of the Pandects."

PART II.

Jurisprudence is the knowledge of laws, their reasons, and their sources. Knowledge of laws and their sources constitutes the history of the law. Knowledge of laws and their reasons constitutes the philosophy of law. Without some tincture of this philosophy none can be said to understand the law; "for though a man can tell the law, yet, if he know not the reason thereof, he shall soon forget his superficial knowledge." To discern these reasons, it is indispensable to study the history of the law. The latter furnishes forth the facts, and in them philosophy searches for their reasons. Philosophy does not create, it discovers the true relations of things.

The relation of man to man is expressed in the youth of nations in customs or usages, which embody the national ideas of justice, and in that way express the character of the people. For no custom can prevail in a nation which is repugnant to its sentiments or sense of justice. Manners are the law of a people at this stage of its progress. These are, then, parcel of the national mind; its moral rule, as well as the arbiter of public and private right. Morally they are the people. The Athenians uttered a universal truth, when, abandoning their territory to its invaders, they said that their country was their customs, and these they carried with them in their ships. Nations in all ages have sent forth colonies which voluntarily separated themselves from their places of nativity, but never from their customs. In fact, they cannot; it is a moral impossibility. They cannot separate themselves from themselves. Hence colonies have always transported their native customs to their foreign homes, and have preserved them so far as they could, consistent with the altered relations of external affairs. In regard to the Germans of the mediæval ages, this is equally true. An erroneous inference from this general truth has, however, been made. Their conquests gave them large territories, which were partitioned between themselves and the conquered people. Each man thus became a landlord. But this was altogether a new relation for them, and to which their customs had no reference; for before they crossed the Rhine, private property in land was absolutely and totally unknown to them. Their customs concerned their rights as men, life, liberty, and property in chattels; and even of these they possessed little more than their wagons, cattle, and arms. Until they had conquered the Roman world, they knew nothing of conveyances, much less of devises of lands, — a refinement upon the right of alienation. *Nullum testamentum*, says Tacitus, — their customs were unwritten, — *leges memoria sola et usu tenebant.* After their conquests, they became subject voluntarily to the influence of the laws, and gave a ready obedience to the Christian pontificate of Rome. Their national characteristics disappeared, in a great measure, in a new civilization; their customs were written, and in the language, and discolored with the ideas, of the conquered. So difficult is it to distinguish even in the Salic and Ripuarian codes the native from the Roman element, that this task is still admitted by eminent German scholars to be as yet unaccomplished.

The fact that the Germans before their invasion had no law of real property, is of great consequence in our judicial history. Savigny has demonstrated that the codes of all the tribes consisted, in a great measure, of Roman law, and it has always been admitted that these were interpreted with the aid of that law. Hence the universal prevalence on the Continent of the Civil Law. The Norman customs, however, did not undergo so great modification. For, being the last of the invading tribes, bringing with them their native customs fresh and pure, they could not at once become Gallo-Romans. Nor, indeed, have they yet become so thoroughly imbued with the principles of the Civil Law as the Franks and Burgundians. The Anglo-Normans, insulated, and almost from the time of the conquest of England hostile to the Gallo-Romans, have of course been less deeply impressed with the mixed law of the Continent. But as the Normans had originally no native custom concerning land, they too, necessarily, when they became proprietors, adopted the only law of real estate of which they had any knowledge, — the mixed Gallo-Roman law.

The change from oral and traditionary to written laws is the beginning of legislation. Legislation is not the law, but the expression of the law antecedently existing. The thought was already in the mind and heart of the people. This is a truth in the juridical history of the world. Legislation cannot be other than the authoritative utterance of the thought of a people. The cause of this change from tradition to legislation has always been political. Thus the Twelve Tables were compiled to remedy the diversity between races, — the Patrician and Plebeian. "The state of affairs," says Niebuhr,* "was exactly like that which led to the framing of the statutes of modern Italy. When the German conquerors and the Romans had grown up together into one nation, with a common language and manners, the universal tendency of circumstances was to mould the two classes into civil communities with new rights, in which those previously separate should be blended." Hence these mixed codes of Roman law and national customs. A similar condition of affairs led Alfred and Edward the Confessor to promulgate their codes. These historical instances prove that the change from tradition to legislation was produced, not only by a

* Rome, Vol. II. p. 210.

political, but by the same political cause. And each of these codes, except that of Edward, became, for the people subject to it, *fons omnis publici, privatique juris.*

The diversity of races, which the laws of Edward were intended to obliterate, arose in a new form after the conquest. William consented that the natives should be governed by their own laws; but at the same time published his code for the government of his followers. This state of affairs tended necessarily to perpetuate the diversity, by establishing two coordinate systems of laws; but he gave the administration of both to the Normans. Interest, contempt for a conquered race, ignorance of the native laws, and a knowledge of their own, combined to render the judges utterly regardless of the native laws. A long period elapsed before the races had blended; but the traces of the Anglo-Saxon upon the law were few and slight. Their customs perished with the people who cherished them, as congenial to their manners and constant memorials of their lost freedom. And whilst the native was becoming obsolete, a foreign code was being substituted by judicial legislation.

The next step in the juridical history of modern times is the promulgation of capitularies or statutes made by the sovereign alone. None of these are now referred to in England as authority, except Magna Charta of Henry the Third (A. D. 1225), two hundred years after the conquest. The antecedent capitularies are generally declaratory, and where remedial or amending, they have been directed to the correction of abuses in the administration of the *jus coronæ.* It is apprehended that they have had little influence in the formation of the Common Law.

Although Bracton lived in the reign of Henry the Third, and wrote within a few years after Magna Charta was granted, he mentions it only passingly, and without attaching to it much importance. Indeed, until the Revolution, when Somers and his coadjutors sought justification of their ideas of popular rights in the law, Magna Charta was almost forgotten. And historically it is not true that the celebrated twenty-ninth chapter had for its purpose the extension of the power of the democratic element in the government. It was intended solely to confirm the owners of lands, *liber homo*, in the enjoyment of such rights as they had beforetime possessed. This statute, says Coke, was but a restitution of the Common Law, and his remark concurs with the truth of history. The English Revolution did, however, extend the basis of political organization, and increase the influence of the popular element. But it seems natural to the lawyer to discern in the past the exact prototype of the present, and it is certainly common to deny that the improvement of the law, public and private, is a change of the antecedent law. Development is with many not progress, and such desire the law to be immutable.

The English Revolution made no change in the law of private property. In like manner, the American Revolution affected only the public law. The tenacity with which every branch of the great Germanic race maintains its primitive customs has always been remarked. The Normans and their descendants have adhered faithfully to their customs in relation to lands, which they adopted in the Middle Ages. Their law of real estate is altogether customary. No code nor statute establishes our system of real estate. Yet in the lapse of nine hundred years, diversified by every incident that can befall a people in prosperous or adverse fortune, — advancing from comparative barbarism to the height of civilization, — changing dynasties, — pendulating from the tyranny of the Tudors to the anarchy of the Barebones Parliament, *indoctissimum genus indoctissimorum hominum*, — not one principle of the law of real estate has been altered. The Justinian of the English law restored the customary law by the statute *de donis*, and the tyrannical Henry the Eighth attempted to lop off that foreign graft in the Common Law, uses. Legislation, with few exceptions, has been confined to the accidental, and has not touched the essentials of the Common Law. Thus, the statute of frauds merely establishes the kind of evidence necessary to prove contracts in certain cases. The statute of wills extends the special customary law to the whole realm. The Habeas Corpus act gave another remedy for illegal imprisonment. Nor has legislation altered in a single particular conveyances at Common Law, but has increased indirectly their number. So the family relations remain, with their incidents, as they were in the earliest periods.

This review shows that the Common Law presents for our investigation a continuity of doctrine, which binds the present to the past, — a chain of rules unbroken by revolutions, not blurred by codification, — in short, a body of original facts. Without the immutability of the Jewish law, it has been stable, amidst the changes of society. It has participated in great revolutions, without being a passing incident in the life of the nation. It is not an episode in the life, it is the life itself of the nation. It is stable, because its principles are founded upon truth; it is capable of amelioration, because that is of the nature of humanity. It must, then, have a philosophy.

THE

THEORY OF THE COMMON LAW.

CHAPTER I.

THE STATE.

THE State is a person, and possesses as its property one territory. As this one civil person consists of all the citizens, so its property consists of all the individual property of the citizens. It is *una persona, unicum patrimonium.* This unity of the person and property of the state is expressed by the Common Law in the maxim, that all lands were originally granted out by the sovereign, and are therefore holden, either mediately or immediately, in fee. The sovereign reserved the *dominium* and ultimate property in the lands, and the grantee acquired only the use and profits.* Thus the right to the soil was separated from the right to the use and profits. In apprehension of law, the state holds the soil of the whole territory as one estate. This idea was not peculiar to the feudal law.† It prevailed univer-

---

* 2 Bl. Com. 51; 1 Co. Litt. 915.

† The generality of the writers on the feudal law seem to consider this fiction, the unity of the state, as the characteristic of that law. Even the learned Vico, whose merits as a philosophical historian are univer-

sally on the Continent, among the German tribes who conquered the Gallo-Roman provinces. Cæsar states, that before their irruption into Gaul they had no private estates in land; "neque quisquam agri modum certum, aut fines proprios." * The territory occupied by them belonged to the tribe, and was repartitioned annually to prevent even local attachments. In like manner Rome held the sovereignty over her conquered provinces. The possessors or tenants, whether Roman citizens or subjects, held their lands *in bonis*, as usufructs, and without that participation in political rights which enabled the citizen to hold lands within the proper territory of the city, *ex jure quiritium*. The latter, known as one of the *res mancipi*, corresponded to the legal estate of the Common Law, and was in the same sense distinguished from the usufruct. Thus Cicero applies the distinction, "ergo fructus est tuus, mancipium illius." † Lucretius more eloquently and accurately says:

> "Vita mancipio nulli datur, omnibus usui." ‡

This idea of the unity of the territory, being common both to the Germans and Romans, was adopted as the basis of the treaties between them previous to the fifth century. Thus, in A. D. 268, the Franks received lands upon the banks of the Rhine, on condition of defending that frontier from barbarian inva-

---

sally acknowledged, has fallen into this error, and, as a consequence, his speculations, always surprising for their novelty and very frequently profound, do not uncover the features of that system. He considers every people as holding its territory in fee of the Great Ruler of the world. That is not more true of feudal England than of Rome. Yet the latter had no knowledge of the feudal law; it arose many centuries after its territory had become the spoil of nations. See Vico, Philosophy of History, Vol. II. ch. 5.

* Comm. 6. 22. † De Div. 7. 29. ‡ 3. 984.

sion and of serving as auxiliaries in the Roman army. Military service was the only rent that, from their previous migratory and predatory habits, they were capable of paying for the use of the lands. On the eastern frontier the same course was adopted; indeed, the Empire, assailed at every point by barbarous tribes, was compelled to employ some of them in its defence. Such also was the tenure of the Salic territory in the early period of the Middle Ages, and for that reason transmissible only to male heirs. Therefore, whilst those tribes in amity with Rome had the use and profits of their lands, the sovereignty termed *dominium populi Romani* by Gaius and *imperium* by Justinian — indicative of the different forms of government — belonged to the *civitas* or state.

It would not be difficult to collect from history numerous other instances of the prevalence of this idea. Indeed, so generally has it been adopted as the foundation of political and territorial organization, that it is one of the points of similarity between the general outlines of theology and jurisprudence.* Hence, too, the jurisconsults of antiquity — theologians, jurists, and philosophers at once — comprehended under the word Justice all the relations of man to man and to God. And therefore they defined jurisprudence to be *divinarum atque humanarum rerum notitia, justi atque injusti scientia.*

This idea being the basis of the political and territorial organization of the whole state, its effects must necessarily be discoverable, in a greater or less degree, in every part of the legal system of that state.

---

* 4 Leibnitz, 185, Duten's ed.; Selden, De Jure, &c.; Collatio. R. & M. leg.

It is not possible that any people should live under a public law which is antagonistical to the private law. The reasons are too palpable to require any elucidation. Therefore, in treating of the private law, altogether to discard consideration of the public, is to neglect that element by which the private law exists. For instance, trial by jury in private causes we value highly; but no one could imagine that it would be valuable in a despotism. The form might survive, but not the life, and it would probably be merely an instrument of oppression. We shall, however, no further notice the public law than is absolutely necessary for the exposition of the private. It will be found that in proportion as the state tends towards unity or centralization, as it is now generally termed, so are the people free or not; and in the same proportion is the security of their rights of property.

In the Common Law, as will hereafter be shown, the idea of the unity of person and of property is applied practically, and with controlling power, to every relation that can arise between the grantor and the grantee of lands, — considered either as persons alone, or as persons in connection with property. Whatever may be the quantity or quality of an estate, — into what number soever of parts it may be divided, — however numerous may be the tenants, — their relations depend upon this principle. They exist, as Bracton says,* *per juris unitatem.* This unity is termed by Blackstone "a fiction of tenure," but, like all other legal facts, it will be found potential in the law, rigorous, and peremptory, admitting no con-

* Fol. 66, 76.

tradiction and suffering no modification. It is the foundation, not only of the public political and territorial law, but of private property, of *status*, of family rights, of courts and their rules of procedure; in short, an exposition of it, as applied to the law of England, is the philosophy of the Common Law.

CHAPTER II.

CIVIL PERSON.

THE state is represented in the person of its chief magistrate, who is at the same time a member of it. Thus the king or president possesses two kinds of rights, a university of rights as a corporation, and individual rights as a man. As the former become more and more confounded with the latter, so government advances towards some form of monarchy. A bishop also is a sole corporation, but the man holding the office has also his individual rights. The word *person* neither according to its accurate meaning nor in law is identical with man. A man may possess at the same time different classes of rights. On the other hand, two or more men may form only one legal person, and have one estate, as partners or corporators. Upon this difference of rights between the person and the man, the individual and the partner, corporator, tenant in common, and joint tenant, depends the whole law of these several classes. The same person has perfect power of alienation, of forming contracts, of disposing by last will and testament of his individual estate, but not of the corporate, nor of his own share in it, unless such power be expressed or implied in the contract by which the university of rights and duties is created. The same distinction divides all public from private property, and distinguishes the cases in which the corporation or civil person may sue from those in which the individual alone can be the party; — although there are instances in which the injury complained of may, in reference to the difference of character, be such as to authorize the suit to be instituted either by the civil person or the individual, or by both. Thus, violence to the person may be punished either as a wrong to the state or to the individual.

The true meaning of the word *person* is also exemplified in the matter of contracts. It is said, generally, that all persons may contract; but that is not true in the sense that all human beings may contract. Thus, a married woman, an infant, a lunatic, cannot contract. Again, a slave of mature age, sound intellect, with the consent of his master, cannot make a contract binding on himself, although as an agent he may bind his master. These matters are important only as they serve clearly to show that the civil person may have rights distinct from those which he possesses as an individual; — and that his rights or duties as an individual may consequently become opposed to his rights and duties as a civil person. Thus, a partnership of three persons may own, for example, a moiety of a ship, and one of them the other moiety. In case of a difference between them as to its use, the rights of the one as a partner, and his right as an individual owner of another moiety, are directly opposed. In order, therefore, in any case, to perceive the application of a rule of law, it must be considered whether the person or the individual, or both, is the possessor of the right. For it may be asserted as absolutely true, that the rights of the man are not recognized by that law which is termed the municipal. It recognizes them only as they grow out of, or are consistent with, his character as a civil person. In other words, this is the distinction between the Common Law and the law of nature. Nor is this a fanciful distinction, inasmuch as the rudest tribes, as well as the most civilized nations, have always distinguished between the rights and duties of their members, and of those who were not members of the body politic. Even after the philosophical jurists of antiquity had polished and improved the jurisprudence of aristocratic republican Rome by the philosophy of the Portico, Cicero, statesman, philosopher, and jurisconsult, exclaims with indignation against the confusion of rights of person that the age witnessed: "In urbem nostrum est infusa peregrinitas; nunc vero etiam *braccatis* et *transalpinis* nationibus ut nullum veteris leporis vestigium appareat." *

The Common Law, as well as the Civil, recognizes as a person an unborn child, when it concerns its interests either as to life or property. "Qui in utero est perinde ac si in rebus humanis esset, custoditur, quotiens de commodis ipsius partus quæritur." And both systems provide the same remedies to protect the child and those with whom its birth may interfere. In case of a limitation to the child of which a woman is now pregnant, if twins should be born, the Common Law gives the estate to the first-born; by our

---

* Epist. ad Fam. 9. 15.

law, they would take moieties. Now, as these rights are acquired before the birth of the child or children, there is a double fiction ; not only in considering the unborn as born, but in distinguishing under the Common Law the eldest from the youngest born. Whilst, therefore, the law regards the unborn as born, yet, to transmit the estate, he must be born as a man, alive and capable of living.

The law does not presume the life or death of an individual; when his existence has been established, his death also must be proved.* But the birth of an individual and the commencement of his character as a person do not necessarily concur. Thus, an alien of any age is not a person, in relation to a contract concerning lands, nor in any case is an infant ; so a woman marrying before she attains her legal maturity may die of old age without having become a person. On the other hand, a person may suffer civil death before physical death; totally, where he becomes a monk; partially, as a penalty for the commission of an infamous crime; and perpetually or temporarily, as in case of outlawry.

---

* Where a person has not been heard of for seven years, and under circumstances which contradict the probability of his being alive, a court may consider this sufficient proof of death (Stark. Ev. 4 pl. 457). The presumptions which arise in such cases do not concern the death of the person, but the time of his death, as where several die by one shipwreck or other casualty. On this point the rules are, — 1st. In case of parents and children, that children below the age of puberty died before, and adult children after, their parents. 2d. Persons not being parents and children, and the rights of one being dependent upon the previous death of the other, this precedent condition must be proved. 3d. If a grant is to be defeated by the act of the grantor, as in case of a *donatio inter virum et uxorem*, or a *donatio mortis causa*, the donor is presumed, in the absence of testimony, to have died first. (See Pothier, Obligations, by Evans, Vol. II. p. 300.)

CHAPTER III.

REMAINDERS.

The unity of estates is exhibited in its simplest form in the fee simple. But in order that its influence in the more subtile portions of the law may be made apparent, the doctrine of vested remainders will be considered. "It is a general rule," says Mr. Fearne, "that every remainder must vest, either during the particular estate, or else at the very moment of its determination. So that, if a lease be made to A for life, and after the death of A, and one day after, the land shall remain to B, this remainder to B is void." Why does the law inexorably demand that the remainders shall vest at the very instant of the determination of the preceding estate? Mr. Fearne states that "this rule was founded upon feudal principles, and was intended to avoid the inconveniences which might arise by admitting an interval when there should be no tenant of the freehold to do the services of the land, or answer to the stranger's præcipe, as well as to preserve an uninterrupted connection between the particular estate and the remainder, which, in the consideration of the law, are but several parts of one whole estate." The feudal principles to which Mr. Fearne refers seem to be those intended to prevent the inconveniences to the lord and the stranger, which would follow from the want of a tenant of the freehold. The explanation might be sufficient, if every remainder necessarily consumed the whole estate remaining after the determination of the preceding estate. Were there no reverter, reversion, or escheat, then, perhaps, the lord might suffer inconvenience. Moreover, when there was no tenant of the freehold able to render service to the lord, — an infant, for example, — the lord might enter and enjoy the profits of the land. The infant was in wardship. If there was no legal tenant, the land reverted to the donor. And in either case, the stranger had a person holding in his own right or *in autre droit*, to answer to his præcipe. Nor is the necessity of an uninterrupted connection between the particular estate and the remainder a sufficient explanation. It involves, in fact, a *petitio principii*. Why was it necessary that this connection should be uninterrupted, even for a moment? Upon what principle does the law declare that a remainder is void, if there be, as in the case above cited, the interval of a day between the particular estate and the remainder? It is manifest that the reason of the rule has no relation to the length of the interval, — a moment is as destructive as a year. In the former case, — a moment, — the want of a tenant could not impose any inconvenience, either upon the lord or a stranger; yet it defeats the remainder as certainly as the interval of a year. The length of the interval was unimportant, and the inconvenience, therefore, was not the reason of the rule. We apprehend that the rule is founded upon reasons very different from those stated by Mr. Fearne.

Without disturbing the learned dust that has incrusted the writings of those system-builders who have maintained that fees were originally held at the will of the lord, and rose by degrees, passing through the stages of leases for years and for life, to the dignity of inheritances, it is sufficient for our purposes to fix ourselves upon that point of time when all agree that estates for life had become general. The tenant for life was bound to render to the lord certain customary services, and any others that might be specially agreed upon between them. On his part, the lord was bound to protect the tenant in the enjoyment of the land, and, in case he was expelled by paramount title, to provide him with another feud. And, as the connection between the lord and the vassal was personal, the latter could not substitute a vassal in his own place, nor the former a lord, without mutual consent. At the termination of the life estate the land reverted to the lord, again to be granted as a feud. It is probable that various motives conspired to induce the lord to grant the land to two or more persons, in succession, for life. Let us suppose the case of a limitation to A for life, and from and after his death to B for life. By the common law, livery of seizin was necessary to give title to a freehold interest in land. When, therefore, the tenant for life took livery of seizin, the remainder-man acquired an inchoate right to the remainder. This right vested in the remainder-man as soon as the particular estate commenced, but it did not authorize him to enter into the possession of the land, even at the death of the tenant for life, without the consent of the lord. "Sciendum est fœudum sine investitura, nullo modo constitui posse." * Now, if the tenant for life forfeited his estate, — and only by forfeiture could he lose it, — it necessarily reverted to the lord: because the remainder-man, not having livery of seizin, could not enter, to exclude the lord, — and livery could not be granted him, as remainder-man, under the original

* Liber Feudorum, tit. 25; 1 Reeves, 154.

agreement, for the tenant for life was not dead. The resumption of the land by the lord was not the acquisition of a new estate, but his restoration to his original estate: for the tenure, or contract of holding, was that the lord might reënter for breach of any condition; being restored to his old estate, the remainder, necessarily, no longer existed. It ceased with the estate upon which it depended. The same principle is found in many other cases, and applied with even greater rigor. Thus, if a man seized of an estate in fee marries, and afterwards the condition is broken, and the lord enters for the breach, he will avoid the wife's title to dower.* So, entry for breach of a condition will defeat all rent-charges, statutes, and judgments.† To prevent, therefore, the failure of the remainder, consequent upon a reverter to the lord of his old estate, *the tenancy for life must, in every case, continue until the moment* when, by the law of the contract, the remainder-man is entitled to demand livery of seizin.

The rule, therefore, is grounded upon the plainest principles of justice. A remainder-man was, in fact and in law, a party with the tenant for life in a contract with the lord. The tenant covenanted to perform certain obligations *in præsenti;* the remainder-man *in futuro*; and the lord contracted with both *in præsenti.* And it is clear that, by the contract, the rights of the remainder-man were dependent upon the fidelity of his coöbligor, the tenant, to his obligations. This was the contract. It was a condition annexed to the contract, — a part of the contract, — that the life estate should be forfeited for certain causes. The contract, in the language of the

* 1 Roll. Abr. 474.

† 1 Rep. 147.

civilians, contained a clause of nullity. We have seen, from Rolle and Coke, that even dower was avoided by a violation of the condition. So, by the Civil Law, if a mortgage was given upon an estate held upon condition, and the covenant or contract by which the estate was held was dissolved by the event of the condition, the mortgage would be defeated.* This is in accordance with the general rule, *Resoluto jure concedentis, resolvitur jus concessum.*† Thus, by both systems, the original proprietor resumed his estate, free from all encumbrances. As it is said by the common lawyers, he was in of his old estate.

The remainder-man was therefore a party with the tenant in a joint contract with the lord. Being a joint contract, and not several and independent, the remainder necessarily commences at the time of the creation of the particular estate; or, in other words, a remainder cannot be created to commence *in futuro*. Hence, too, the interests of the tenant and remainder-man constitute but one estate in judgment of law. These are all the rules of the doctrine of vested remainders.

CHAPTER IV.

FEE.

The principle of unity having been shown to exist with controlling power, not only over the whole territory, but every part of it, and also as entering as a

* Domat, Lib. 1, tit. 1, § 6.

† Dig. 8. 6, fr. 11, s. i.

substantive rule into the more complex portions of the law, its application is further to be considered. It is obvious that the maxim, that all lands are originally holden in fee, has two elements, jurisdiction and property,—the dominion of the state or its sovereignty over the territory. "These, jurisdiction and property, are," says Grotius, "in reference to nations, usually acquired by one act." * Now the distinctive peculiarity of the feudal law was to regard every lord as a sovereign, and every feud as a domain, and, reversing what is in modern times considered the natural order of things, it attributed jurisdiction to the lord by virtue of his possession of land. M. Guizot † marks this singular fact as the constituent element of that system,—the fusion of sovereignty and property; that is, the attribution to the proprietor of the soil, over its inhabitants, of all those rights which constitute what we now call sovereignty, and which at this time are possessed only by the public. Again, Dr. Arnold says,‡ the law of property, of real property especially, and a knowledge of all the circumstances of its tenure and divisions, would throw light upon more than the physical condition of a people; it would furnish the key to some of the main principles prevalent in their society. For instance, the feudal notion that property in land confers jurisdiction, and the derivation of property either from the owner's own sword, or from the gift of the stronger chief whose sword he had aided, not from a regular assignment of society, has more deeply affected the political and social state of the modern nations of Europe. At Rome, as elsewhere among the free governments of the ancient world, property was

* De Jure, Lib. 2, c. 3.
† Hist. Civ. France, Vol. IV. p. 38.
‡ Hist. Rome, ch. 14.

derived from political rights, rather than political rights from property. And we may add, that this is true of the United States. This fusion of jurisdiction and property in lands was the peculiarity of the feudal system. The sovereign granted out the use and profits of the lands to his vassals, but retained sovereignty over them. By virtue of it, he imposed taxes, coined money, made war, sat as a judge in Aula Regis, surrounded with his vassals as a council. So, in like manner, every lord, upon receiving investiture of a fee from his superior, immediately acquired, by attribution of law, the rights of sovereignty over his vassals, and sat as a judge in his baronial court, surrounded by his vassals. Thus we read in Liber Feudorum: * "Si inter duos vassalos de feudo sit controversia, domini sit cognitio et per eum controversia terminetur." The greater barons made war, coined money, imposed taxes, and, in short, exercised all the rights of a sovereign; the smaller were restrained, by their want of the necessary physical power, from asserting these rights in their plenitude. This was the only difference between the greatest and the least of the barons in the feudal age.†

The sovereignty exercised by a baron of any rank over his vassals was twofold; first, by means of his court, and secondly, directly and without its intervention. But in the course of time, as the turbulence of the state subsided, many instances of the latter class were enforced only by means of the court. For instance, the inquest at the suit of the crown to

* Tit. 1, p. 18.

† *Baron* in the feudal age did not mean that the person had a title of honor. He was strictly a landlord. Coke uses the word in a wider sense, as "feoffment to baron and feme," meaning man and wife. *Homo* was a vassal; *liege, ligatus*, bound to a lord.

establish an escheat from want of heirs to the last person seized, has arisen since the feudal systems began to decline. The fact was always notorious, and the land was therefore immediately seized. An instance of this notoriety being sufficient, without further proof, will be found in the case of Dr. Storie,* who was hanged for treason, being notoriously a native. The king, upon the commission of treason by rebellion, or denial of his feudal supremacy, did not, under the ancient Common Law, wait upon the pedetentous pace of the law, but instantly seized the lands of the traitor. The inferior lord, when his vassal denied his tenure, as by doing homage to another lord or attempting to alien his feud, also instantly entered and resumed his old estate. In both cases, — of the king and the lord, — the seizure was justified upon the same ground, that the tenant or vassal had denied his allegiance, and each exercised his right of entry. The right of entry is therefore a portion of the ancient jurisdiction or sovereignty of the owner of the fee.

Furthermore, for the purpose of distinguishing clearly sovereignty or jurisdiction from property, we will analyze a fee simple. Littleton tells us, that a tenant in fee simple is he that hath the lands and tenements to him and his heirs for ever. But neither he, nor any other of our juridical writers, has given an account of a fee without any adjective, — simple, conditional, tail, &c. It is not peculiar to lands, and may be of titles of honor, of offices, incorporeal hereditaments, and also of that species of personal property known as annuities. It is not the use and profits of land, nor necessarily annexed to them; for

* Dyer, fo. 300, b. pl. 38.

if lands be limited to A, and the heirs of his body, the fee continues in the donor, but the use and profits are the inheritance of A. It is not assignable nor divisible, nor can we conceive of its partition into shares.* Thus two tenants in common of an inheritance have one fee, but undivided moieties of the use and profits, but neither nor both can transfer the fee. When they transfer the use and profits with the consent of the lord, the law attributes to the donee the sovereignty or fee. Its existence is shown in the right of entry. As the king reserved sovereignty or jurisdiction, or, more properly, as it did not pass from him, so does the donor still continue to possess it, whenever he creates an estate of inheritance less than simple. Whenever the tenant violates his tenure, by treason or by alienation of his life estate in fee, the donor, whether king or tenant in fee simple, may exercise his jurisdiction and resume his estate.

The manifest object of attributing to the lord this right of entry, or jurisdiction, was to enforce the faithful performance by the tenant of the duties in-

* By the 32 Hen. 8, c. 34, the grantee of a reversion may take advantage, in certain cases, of a condition broken; that is, a right of entry was given to him. By the Common Law, only the donor and his heirs could enter. Coke states a number of consequences of this change of the Common Law, but in language which, though intelligible, is incorrect. Thus, that "a condition may be divided by act of law or by the wrong of the lessee." Here he clearly means that *a* right of entry for breach of the condition is given to each grantee, where by act of law the land which was subject to one condition passes to several grantees, or where in such case one lessee of a part has violated his contract, and the other lessee has not. The right of entry, a condition, a power, are merely legal entities, of which we cannot conceive a partition; nor can it pass from one to another, as a piece of land may. But a right of entry may be delegated, that is, the party having it may appoint another to make the entry. Or, where the entry is made, he may afterwards approve and adopt it. Spencer's case, 3 Rep. 16; 1 Smith's Leading Cases, 75; 2 Strange, 1128. "Coke, it must be confessed, was sadly negligent of style," says Lord Campbell.

cumbent upon him. As it is the power of punishing wrong, it is also necessarily the power of protecting right. Both these objects are combined in the office of trustees to preserve contingent remainders and uses. They have the right of entry upon the particular estate where the tenant attempts to destroy the contingent interests, and by their entry to preserve them. It is apparent, therefore, that the right of entry or fee is the last remnant of the jurisdiction that the feudal law attributed to property. Jurisdiction, fee, right of entry, is the ligament which binds the whole territory of the state and the several parts of it together in unity.

That the word *fee* originally signified only the property in lands is certain; the jurisdiction exercised by the lord was termed his sovereignty. Thus Coke terms the abbot of a monastery the sovereign of the house.* But, in the progress of time, the word *sovereign* came to be applied exclusively to the king, and jurisdiction ceased to be distinguished in language from the fee. Thus fee was made to comprehend jurisdiction, as well as the property. This confusion continues to the present time, and we use that word, in the present instance, for want of another familiar to us, and expressive of the attribute of property.†

* Vol. I. p. 493.

† In the feudal age, after the terms of the contract between the lord and the vassal were agreed upon, the latter was invested with seizin by livery, and then, as we have seen, the law attributed jurisdiction, fee, or sovereignty. The latter, sovereignty, first ceased to be prominent; then, as the feudal system declined, livery or investiture became a mere form, and now even that form is *generally* not observed, and in many of the States is altogether abolished. It is not surprising, therefore, that the remnant of sovereignty and of livery which still exists in the law should have been neglected by modern writers. In a subsequent chapter, we shall have occasion to show the very important consequences of seizin, even at the present time, in the doctrine of descent.

CHAPTER V.

SCINTILLA JURIS.

FEE or sovereignty has no element of property, although by the feudal law it is the attribute of property. It exists only in legal apprehension, and is neither assignable, devisable, nor divisible. Now it is believed that the neglect to distinguish between the fee used in the sense of sovereignty, and fee as meaning property, has led both writers and judges into grave errors. For example, in Chudleigh's case, the limitation was to the use of A for life, remainder to his sons successively in tail. Before A had a son, the feoffees enfeoffed him in fee simple. The court held, that, by virtue of the statute of uses, all the seizin, estate, and possession of the feoffees were in the *cestui que use in esse;* and that a possibility of seizin continued in the trustees, to support the uses as they should arise. This is the much vexed question of the *scintilla juris.*

Mr. Fearne has shown that this doctrine is irreconcilable with the statute of uses. But, with the utmost deference for the opinions of that eminent lawyer, it is believed, that, however complete may be his refutation of the doctrine of the court, his own explanation is equally untenable. Mr. Butler states it thus: "That by the statute the whole seizin is at once completely divested out of the feoffees, and that, when the contingent uses become vested, the use is executed in the person to whom it is limited, not in consequence of any seizin then accruing to the feoffees, but in consequence of the lands being originally conveyed to them with a *liability* in consequence of the statute to be attracted to the uses." The statute was intended to eradicate uses, but not to prevent the creation nor to destroy contingent interests. Its purpose was to lop off from the law those foreign grafts, uses and trusts. The courts, to preserve these contingent estates, resorted to the *scintilla juris.* Mr. Fearne suggests "a liability to be attracted to the uses," annexed to the land.

Now it is as difficult to comprehend this "liability" as the *scintilla juris ;* and the latter phrase has this advantage, that it is used by Bracton, and the former has no authority for it. It is true, however, that Bracton uses it to express emphatically the entire absence of right, — "nullum jus haberet nec juris scintillam ejiciendi." * Moreover, Mr. Fearne reverses the rule of the law, that the land attracts the fee, and holds that the contingent use attracts the land. But the statute changed the equitable into a legal estate; it did not and could not make the contingent a vested use; much less confer upon the contingent *cestui que* the enjoyment of the use and profits. Until they became vested, even considering them as merely legal, and not as equitable interests, the fee or jurisdiction continued in the feoffees, and was not assignable by them. That jurisdiction, fee, or right of entry was in itself sufficient to support the uses, without resort to the imaginary *scintilla juris*, which contradicted the statute or the liability, which has no authority for its use. The statute, then, has its full force, and the seizin estate and possession are trans-

---

* Lib. 4, fol. 183, c. 18.

ferred to the *cestui que use in esse.* When the other uses arise, they are supported by the right of entry. The feoffment by the feoffees was therefore a nugatory act. Nothing continued in them but jurisdiction or right of entry, which is not assignable. Nor can the right of entry be barred by a feoffment,* for at Common Law anciently actual livery was necessary, and though subsequently, in the reign of Elizabeth, it was held that a feoffment by a mere wrongdoer in possession conveyed a fee, yet in the principal case the feoffees had not possession; it was in the eldest son A. If, therefore, it be admitted that trustees to preserve contingent uses may bar their right of entry, it is clear that a feoffment is not the appropriate instrument.

That the court confounded sovereignty or fee with something of which seizin might be predicated, is palpable. Whereas, the feoffees had neither seizin estate nor possession, but merely a right of entry, that was not assignable, and which we cannot conceive as passing from them to the tenant. The liability which Mr. Fearne suggests as a convenient substitute for the *scintilla juris*, is equally incorrect. He fastens upon the land as a kind of lien what his opponents conceived to be a possession, or possibility of it. In fact, the court and himself mean the same thing, but they look at it on different sides; the court thought the feoffees had a possibility of right to the land, he thought that the lands were subject to a liability or duty. Neither, therefore, was correct; the feoffees had only a *facultas*, power, or right of entry, and they needed no more to support the contingent uses.

---

* 4 Cruise, 287.

It was not an interest, but just the identical right that the state has to seize the lands of a traitor, or that the donor and his heirs have to enter upon breach of a condition, or resume an estate after the death of the last special heir, to whom it has been limited.

It is because the fee is jurisdiction, and not property, that a remainder cannot be created after a fee conditional. It cannot be divided, and therefore tenants in common and joint tenants have only one fee; although during their cotenancy they may enjoy the use and profits in different proportions. When their shares are divided and are taken in severalty, the law attributes to each its own fee or jurisdiction.

CHAPTER VI.

CONTINGENT REMAINDERS.

It is requisite that the remainder be in the party to whom it is limited at the time of the livery. "This is regularly true; but yet it hath divers exceptions": * these are contingent remainders. When it is said that the remainder must be in the grantee at the time of the livery, it is evident that nothing more is thereby meant, than that the right to the enjoyment of the use and profits after the death of the tenant then begins. In the mean time they belong to the tenant of the freehold. Now, where that right

* 2 Co. Litt. 150.

is limited to an uncertain person, the rule that the right must be in the party to whom it is limited as soon as the livery is made, cannot be observed. Hence some persons, to fulfil the letter of the rule that the remainder must pass out of the donor and be in the donee, insist that, so long as the person is uncertain, the fee is in abeyance. It would be sufficient to refer to Mr. Fearne for a refutation of this notion, but that his argument implies that fee has some element of property. Stating the proposition correctly, that nothing remains to the donor, after he has disposed of the use and profits, but jurisdiction, there can be no pretence for the doctrine of abeyance.

When a lord or tenant in fee simple has created a freehold interest, with a contingent remainder over, he has divested himself in favor of the tenant of the use and profits, and has nothing more than jurisdiction and the ultimate property. His fee can no more be in abeyance than that of the state would be if it created a similar estate. The donor has a right of entry to protect the contingent interest, or, if he has created none, to protect his reversion or reverter. It can be used only against the tenant, and not against the remainder-man, whether vested or contingent. It is for the benefit of the latter, and hence its mere existence is sufficient to support these limitations. From the fact that it is the duty of the trustees to exercise the right of entry to preserve contingent remainders, springs their liability to punishment for its abuse, or non-user. The duty which the trustees owe to the contingent remainder-man, although an uncertain person, gives that person, when known, a right; so that, in fact, there is between the trustees and the remainder-man a contract. That the uncertainty as to the person who may have the right to enforce a contract does not negative its existence, is shown in many cases. Thus, where a person binds himself by his obligation to pay another, his heirs, executors, or administrators, £100, upon the death of the obligee, he may or may not have executors; and either way, before his death, it is uncertain upon whom will devolve the right to enforce the contract. When the suit is instituted, it is not as upon a new right accruing subsequent to the death of the obligee, but upon the original contract.

In case of a limitation to the heirs of B, it is certain that, at his death, he will have heirs. These would, therefore, by the terms of the limitation, take the estate, although the heirs of B should not be in existence at the death of B, as if he survived the first taker. There is nothing in the contract, or words of limitation, to negative this view. But it is certain that the heirs of B will not take the estate unless he dies before the tenant, and during the continuance of the particular estate. The remainder takes effect, provided that the condition upon which it is limited is performed during the life estate. This rule, which inexorably demands that the remainder should vest, at latest, *eo instanti* with the death of the first taker, is the public law, and no part of the contract between the donor and donee. The former cannot vary it or introduce any modifications of it. The public law requires that its fundamental principle, the unity of estates, should be observed.

But we allude to this subject at this time more particularly to notice that the vested and contingent remainders differ in this respect, that the latter are dependent upon a condition. The uncertainty of the vesting of the contingent remainder is because that event, its vesting, is suspended by a condition which may not happen or be performed during the continuance of the particular state. Mr. Fearne uses the phrase "event or condition," in his definition of a contingent remainder, and in all his rules except the third, *event*. But it is evident that the definition is properly a summing up of his rules. Moreover, it will be seen, upon examination, that his four classes can, without prejudice to their accuracy, be stated in another form of words, which will admit the use of one or other of the four phrases which, according to Coke, are peculiarly expressive of conditions. This is noticeable only because it lays open the true elements of the doctrine of contingent remainders. The law of these limitations is the doctrine of conditions, controlled by the principle of the unity of estates. Thus, an estate may be limited to A for life, and from and ten years after his death to the heirs of B, without conflict with any rule of the doctrine of conditions; but such a limitation would be void, because it would sever the unity of the estate.*

These exceptions, contingent remainders, are admitted into the law, therefore, upon intelligible principles. The feudal principle which still inhabits our law requires that the interests of the tenant and remainder-man should be united. It would defeat the jurisdiction of the donor, if, when the tenant forfeited, the remainder-man, whom we have seen to be a joint contractor with the tenant, did not also lose his right; and this would follow if another interest, independent of the freehold, intervened between those

* 4 Reeves, 509.

two estates. But so long as the unity of the estate is preserved, the remainder may be made to depend upon any limitation, condition, proviso, that the donor may dictate. *Cujus est dare, ejus est disponere.* The condition annexed to the remainder only renders it uncertain during the previous estate. The tenant is certain at the time of the happening of the condition. Where the condition, however, not only renders the limitation over uncertain, but also the duration of the life estate itself, it is a conditional limitation, according to Mr. Fearne, and void at Common Law.

CHAPTER VII.

CONDITIONS.

THE doctrine of contingent remainders is, as we have seen, the application to remainders of the law of conditions, circumscribed as to the time of their performance by the public law. "Conditio dicetur cum quid in casum incubum qui potest tendere aut esse aut non esse confertur." * When coupled with an interest in property, as in case of a remainder, then the definition of the Civil Law is more accurate. "Conditio appellatur, eventus a cujus futura et incerta existentia, pendere obligationem aut ultimam voluntatem, contrahentibus testatori ve placuit." † Pothier defines it thus: "A condition is the case of

---

* 2 Co. Litt. 3.

† Regula Juris, 51.

a future event which may or may not happen, and upon which the obligation is made to depend." *

The rules of conditions are not exclusively confined to the law, but are equally applicable to every moral science. They constitute a part of logic, and when applied to legal propositions, of legal logic. A condition neither affirms nor denies any proposition, but suspends it. It is the significant of doubt, rendering the proposition or limitation to which it is annexed uncertain. The conditions which concern contingent remainders, or other such interests, must be distinguished from those conditions usually termed implied, not only because the former are expressed, but because they differ materially in their natures. An implied condition may alter or defeat an estate, but never creates an estate. They seem rather to be essential parts of a contract, — unexpressed terms of it, — than accidents. Thus, no life estate or fee conditional can be created without an implied condition that the donor may enter for breach of it. Every ante-nuptial settlement implies that the conveyance shall be void in case the marriage does not happen. Moreover, these conditions do not suspend the limitations of estates to which they are annexed.

The use of logic is, among other things, to determine the right use of terms, and thus to point out the abuse of them, and also to distinguish between terms rightly used, and the natures and properties of the different terms. The application of logic to legal questions has been admirably illustrated by Mr. Fearne, in his treatise on Contingent Remainders. After defining such a limitation, and stating four

---

* Oblig. 1. c. 3.

classes of contingent remainders, he proceeds to show the true meaning of these words. In his third section, he distinguishes conditional limitations from contingent remainders, which Mr. Douglas had confounded, and in the remaining part of the chapter he shows that, by abuse of terms, vested have been mistaken for contingent remainders. In short, he shows by his criticism, that the words which were supposed to create conditions did not, and therefore that the remainders were vested. This discussion occupies the greater part of his treatise, and, as has been observed by Mr. Butler in his preface, "No work on any branch of science affords a more beautiful instance of analysis."

Mr. Fearne continues his logical criticism, and shows that certain words seem to imply conditions, but that these are false conditions, — not conditions. Thus, the definition of a condition requires that the condition should render the limitation uncertain, not impossible. Hence, if an event must happen, as death, the limitation is not uncertain, and therefore is unconditional; if it cannot happen, then it is impossible, and the limitation is unconditional. In the former case, the limitation over is vested and valid, in the latter the limitation is void. Again, under the head of impossibilities, are conditions against law; it would be an absurdity to term that a legal condition, which can be performed only by an illegal, immoral, or indecent act. The definition also requires that the event of the condition should render the limitation certain or uncertain; that the event should cause the limitation to take effect, or to be defeated. Therefore it cannot create or destroy a part of the limitation. It requires that the condition should produce certainty or uncertainty as to that limitation. Hence it must create or defeat that limitation, not another, and a different one. A condition is the significant of doubt, and merely an accident annexed to the limitation; therefore, if the event is an infringement of the limitation, it is inconsistent with it and cannot be annexed to it, and therefore the condition is void; as that upon a certain event a fee simple shall not be alienable.

These are some of the principal rules of logic, and have been noted with reference to the treatise on Contingent Remainders. In that work the examples and illustrations will readily be found. To attempt to epitomize it, would be to do it injustice, as it contains no matter superfluous to the practical lawyer or the legal speculatist.

Conditions are either precedent or subsequent. This division is founded upon a regard to the consequences of them, and not upon their location in the deed, nor upon their terms. They are precedent when they are the beginning, and subsequent when they are the ending, of a limitation. Yet a condition may be at the same time both precedent and subsequent, the beginning and the end. For instance, in the case of a conditional limitation, the same condition in reference to the previous estate is subsequent and its end, and in reference to the limitation over, it is precedent and its beginning. And that the limitation over is a conditional limitation is because of the uncertainty that the condition will be performed; if that was certain, then it would mark the natural termination of the particular estate, and the limitation over would be a remainder.

4*

CHAPTER VIII.

RELATION.

Ordinarily a contract upon condition specifies the time at or before which the condition must be performed; in the absence of such specification, the law fixes it. But in reference to contingent remainders the law does not leave it optional with the donor to specify the time, but demands inexorably that the condition be performed during the life of the tenant of the particular estate. At the moment of his death, the remainder must be capable of vesting in possession; although by the contract the condition may be required to be performed before that period. In like manner, the heir must be capable of taking at the time of his death, as if, being heir apparent, he becomes *civiliter mortuus*, the estate will not devolve upon him. Now, the tenant of a particular estate has one estate, and as to him the remainder-man has one estate. Yet both, by reason of the jurisdiction of the donor, have as to him one estate. The relations, however, of the tenant and remainder-man towards each other, are, as we have seen, determined by contract, but their relations to the donor depend upon jurisdiction. As to each other, the tenant has only the enjoyment of the use and profits before they pass or devolve upon the remainder-man. Such, too, is the relation of the ancestor and heir; setting aside the consequences of the jurisdiction of the ancestor, and having regard only to his enjoyment of the use and profits, and their devolution upon the heir. Both the heir and remainder-man obtain the use and profits at the death of the party who previously enjoyed them. The seizin of the tenant and that of the ancestor are the seizin of the heir and remainder-man; disseizin reduces them to a right of entry, and that being tolled to a right of action.

It is to be observed, that the right of an heir does not begin with the death of the ancestor. For the seizin of the ancestor, not his possession, gives seizin to the heir, and seizin was obtained at the commencement of the estate. It is a rule of the Common Law, that no inheritance can vest in possession till the ancestor is previously dead. Before that time, the person who is next in the line of succession is called heir apparent or heir presumptive. Heirs apparent are such whose right of inheritance is indefeasible, provided they outlive the ancestor; heirs presumptive are such whose right of inheritance may be defeated.* Nor is this rule of referring the right back to a time anterior to the death of the ancestor, limited to the case of heirs. Thus the remainder is referred back to the commencement of the particular estate. The donor of a fee conditional which has reverted to him by failure of issue, is in of his old right, not of a new estate. A wife's right to dower is referred back to the marriage, and will prevail against a subsequent charge imposed on the estate. Coke, after stating a case of a rent charge being displaced by the right of dower, remarks: "In which case two notable things are to be observed. First, albeit the dower be by *relation* or fiction of law above the rent, yet she shall not have her entire rent out of the residue, for a rela-

---

* 3 Cruise, 349.

tion or fiction of law shall never work a wrong, or charge a third person; but *in fictione juris, semper est equitas.*" These fictions, however much they may startle the minds of those undisciplined in the reason of the law, are legal truths, admitting no contradiction.

Further illustration of this fiction will be found in conveyances by Common Law and by custom of copyhold. The surrenders of copyholds are construed as deeds and conveyances at Common Law. If a copyholder surrender to the use of his will, and devises to a stranger, and then dies, the devisee by his admittance takes as of the day of the surrender. So where at Common Law a person, having made a will of lands, acquires afterwards other lands, and dies, not having republished his will, the devisee takes as of the time of making the will, and therefore does not obtain the lands after acquired.* So, says Lord Chief Baron Gilbert, in his book on Tenures, there is no rule better founded in law, reason, and convenience, than this, that all the several parts and ceremonies necessary to complete a conveyance shall be taken together as *one act*, and operate from the substantial parts by *relation.* Livery related to the feoffment, — enrolment, to the bargain and sale, — a recovery, to the deed which leads the uses; so admittance relates to the surrender. The retroactive effects of grants are seen also in the case of an alien, who has issue; that issue is not inheritable to his father, but if he be naturalized that issue may inherit. But if one be made denizen, the issue that he hath afterwards shall be heir to him, but no issue that he had

* 5 Cruise, 575.

before.* Again, "There is a great diversity as to the forfeiture of land between an attainder of felony by outlawry upon appeal and upon an indictment; for in case of an appeal, the defendant shall forfeit no lands but such as he had at the time of the outlawry pronounced; but in case of an indictment, such as he had at the time of the felony committed."† So that, if he had given away his lands, in the latter case they would still be forfeitable.‡

CHAPTER IX.

HEIR. — THE RULE IN SHELLEY'S CASE.

Closely connected with the doctrine of remainders is the rule in Shelley's case. Where a limitation is made to A for life, remainder to the heirs or heirs of the body of B, A has only a life estate. But if the limitation be to A for life, remainder to the heirs or heirs of the body of A, he has an inheritance. The former is, and the latter is not, a remainder. The only reason given by our writers for this difference is, that the latter limitation is within the rule in Shelley's case. Mr. Fearne states it thus: "Wherever an ancestor takes an estate of freehold, and a remainder is thereon limited mediately or immediately in the same conveyance to his heirs or to the heirs of his body, such remainder is executed in the ancestor." Why? Neither the great argument of Mr. Justice

---

* 1 Co. Litt. 104. † 3 Co. Litt. 609. ‡ 3 Rep. 82.

Blackstone in Perrin and Blake, nor the admirable criticism of Mr. Fearne on that case and the rule itself, enlightens us as to its origin. It is too important, however, not to receive careful consideration.

An estate in fee did not originally pass an estate in the same sense as we now use it. For instance, where an estate was granted to a person and his heirs, he could not alienate it without the consent of the heir.* The heir took by purchase, and not by descent. This was equally true of base or qualified and conditional fees. But before the time of Glanville (A. D. 1189), tenants in fee simple, as we now term them, had acquired the power, but tenants in fee conditional still continued unable, to alienate. When Bracton wrote (A. D. 1268), the latter had also obtained the right of alienation. This, it is universally admitted, was produced by judicial legislation. To correct this novelty, and restore the ancient Common Law, the statute *de donis* was enacted (A. D. 1285).† It was merely declaratory, and enjoined that the will of the donor *secundum formam chartæ*, which had beforetime been disregarded, should thereafter be observed. It is at this point that our law diverges from the English law. Fees tail with them correspond exactly to the fees conditional of the Common Law; at all events, if they do not, it is because courts have adopted principles irreconcilable with the statute *de donis*. In this country, fees conditional at Common Law are recognized, and at the same time the rule in Shelley's case. It is totally unnecessary to resort to the idea of the performance of a condition

---

* 3 Kent, 403.

† 1 Burr. 105.

by the ancestor to execute the remainder in him, for the limitation is within the very letter and spirit of the rule in Shelley's case. And to apply this rule in the performance of a condition to fees conditional at Common Law is an error, inasmuch as juridical history and English legislation prove that where a limitation was made at Common Law to A and the heirs of the body, they took by purchase, and not by descent,— and upon the death of the ancestor might recover the estate by a suit at law.

However, juridical writers have stated that they are conditional fees for this reason, — that it was a condition implied, that, if the ancestor begot heirs of his body, he should have an inheritance. As well might it be said, that, where an estate was granted to A and his heirs, it was upon condition that he should have an inheritance if he had heirs. For by the ancient Common Law, as we have seen, he could not alienate if he had heirs, and such, the statute *de donis* declares, was the Common Law of conditional fees. In these cases, the words *heirs* and *heirs of the body* only determined the quantity of estate that passed from the donor, and in both cases, upon the failure of heirs, general or special, the land reverted to the donor. This is the only conclusion that can be drawn from Bracton, who wrote (A. D. 1268) seventeen years before the enactment of the statute *de donis*. He is, therefore, the latest authority on this subject. After stating a coarcted limitation to particular heirs, he says, "Si autem, nullos tales hæredes habuerit, revertatur illa terra, ad donatorem per conditionem tacitam etiam si nulla mentio in donatione habeatur."* Which

* Lib. 2.

may be translated thus: "If the tenant shall have no heirs of his body, the land reverts to the donor by an implied condition, *even* if none be expressed in the deed." Again, he states that, as the remoter heirs are excluded, if the heirs of the body fail, the land reverts to the donor by a condition expressed or implied; — "in quo casu, cum omnes hæredes remotiores excluduntur, sit terra reversura ad donatorem per conditionem tacitam vel expressam si tales hæredes defecerint sicut adjicit donator in charta donationis." The condition was not to enlarge the estate of the tenant, but to cause it to revert to the donor. In other words, the condition was not that he should have a fee upon the birth of issue, but that if he did not have issue it should revert to the donor, and if he did have heirs it should go to them *secundum formam chartæ*. Plowden states the rule with accuracy in the following sentence: "The fee simple absolute was where land was given to a man and his heirs; the other, to the heirs of his body, which was also fee simple." * (Why, then, was the birth of issue not a condition in both cases?) "But in this case (fee conditional) there was a condition annexed to it, that, if he died without heirs, the land should revert to the donor." † Clearly the condition was for the benefit of the donor, and whereby he might regain his old estate, and not for the benefit of the donee, and to enlarge his estate. We apprehend, therefore, that it was upon some other ground than the performance of a condition by the donee, that the judges determined that upon the birth of issue the limitation to heirs of the body was executed in him. And the

* 235, b.

† 1 P. W. 74.

true ground is, as we have before intimated, the rule in Shelley's case.

Blackstone attributes the interpretation of these limitations adopted by the judges to their sense of the inconveniences of fettered inheritances.* The clamorous demand of the barons for the enactment of the statute *de donis* proves that they did not feel these inconveniences, and they owned nearly every acre in the kingdom. Many attempts were made in the succeeding two hundred years to repeal it,† but it had contributed so much to the increase of the power of the barons, that they always refused their consent. At length, Taltarum's case was got up by Edward the Fourth, and estates tail were defeated by the *astutia* of the judges. An open avowal of the sentiment, that these estates were inconvenient to the crown, as they were insuperable impediments to royal vengeance and rapacity, would have been extremely perilous to the reverend bench. They exhibited their *astutia* by applying to these limitations a rule derived from the Civil Law. The subject deserves examination, not only because of the importance of the rule in Shelley's case, but because it will uncover also the true character of the heir at Common Law, — an inquiry which has been altogether neglected by our juridical writers.

It is certain that, where a limitation was made to the heirs of the body, these were intended to take by purchase, and not by descent. Such was the old Common Law. "But if a man," says Lord Coke, "makes a gift in tail, or a lease for life, the remainder to his

* Vol. I. 112.

† Barr. Stat. 131.

right heirs, this remainder is void, and he hath the reversion in him; for the ancestor during his life beareth in his body in judgment of law all his heirs, and therefore it is truly said that *hæres est pars antecessoris.* And this appeareth in a common case, that if land be given to a man and his heirs, all his heirs are so totally in him as he may give the land to whom he will." * Here, the idea expressed is, that during the life of the ancestor he and his heirs are one person, — *hæres est pars antecessoris,* — the heir is part of him. So the family and the father, in judgment of law, are one; their rights are his, and can only be vindicated, as to other persons, by and through him. So the rights of all the families in a state are so totally in the state that it may dispose of them. The idea of the unity of the father and son, the ancestor and heir, was familiar to the Romans. Cicero, in his philosophic treatise on laws, recognizes it: "Coronam virtute partam, et ei qui peperisset et ejus parenti, sine fraude lex impositam jubet." † On the other hand, the heir *quoadmodo* during the life of the ancestor joined with him in the property. Thus Cicero, in his speech against Verres, says of children, "*Quibus cum vivi* bona nostra partimur." So Justinian: "Sed sui quidem hæredes ideo appellantur, quia domestici hæredes, et vivo quoque patre, *quoadmodo domini* existimantur." ‡ Again, in a play of Terence, a father speaking of his son calls him "meus particeps"; *hæres pars antecessoris.* § The Code states it thus: "Cum et natura pater et filius, eadem esse persona pene intelligan-

---

* 2 Co. Litt. 146.

† 2. 24.

‡ Gaius, 2. 157. Justinian, 2. 19.

§ 6. 26.

tur." Indeed, the word *hæres*, heir, is only another form of *herus*, owner.*

By the adoption of this rule of the Civil Law, that the heir and the ancestor are one, — *hæres pars antecessoris*, — the limitations to the heir were executed in the ancestor. The heir did not, by the Civil Law, acquire the right after the death of the ancestor; he then succeeded to him in the enjoyment of the use and profits. Upon the same principle, the earnings of the child become the property of the father. The latter absorbs all his rights, and his wrongs can only be vindicated by the father. Hence, in the language of Lord Coke, "if land be limited to a man and the heirs of his body, all his heirs are so totally in him as he may give the land to whom he will." The maxim that *nemo est hæres viventis* is strictly applicable to this explanation. *Heir* means, in that maxim, owner. Before the death of the ancestor, he is heir apparent; but in a particular case, as Coke shows,† the heir apparent may also be complete heir and have the use and profits of an estate. He is termed the *hæres astrarius*, ‡ and he takes by descent; for

* De verb. Signi, 22 Pand. 168, s. 108. † 2 Co. Litt. 226.

‡ Ducange, Gloss., v. *Astrum*. The Celtic customs, of which this species of heirship was one, did not recognize the right of the elder brother to take the family residence, *le manoir*. On the contrary, it was the privilege of the younger. Such was also the Gallic custom, to which Cæsar informs us that those of Kent had a strong resemblance. The former say, *L'astre* (the fireplace or hearth) *demeura al puiné*. The law of Wales also, *Frater natu minimus habebit domicilium principale*. Montesquieu as to the Tartars, L. 18, c. 21. The reason given by the writers on the customary laws of the Celts and Gauls is, that these tribes were accustomed to see the elder sons going forth on migratory or predatory excursions, leaving the care of the aged, the women and children, to the younger. It is an unsolved question in history, whence the Celts and Gauls originally brought their customs. Certainly they were *washed*, by the waves of tribes that we call Germans, into France.

if he took by purchase, he would be subject to relief.

The peculiar character of heirship is discoverable in every part of the law, and will be still further developed in the next chapter.*

CHAPTER X.

WARRANTY.

WHERE a limitation was made to the heirs, or heirs of the body, we have seen that the estate in remainder became executed in the ancestor. Now, in case the ancestor sold the estate, he was bound by the feudal law to protect the purchaser in its enjoyment, and in case of eviction, to recompense him with other lands. This was termed a warranty or covenant real, and bound the lands as a lien, into whose hands soever they passed by descent. And as feoffment, fine, exchange, partition, were the only species of conveyance, the feoffer was always bound by an implied warranty, in every sale of lands.† Express warranties could scarcely exist, inasmuch as writing was to the generality an unknown art. Thus, by the ancient Common Law every sale of lands implied a warranty, and so far is identical with the Civil Law. Good faith is the foundation of warranty in both systems.

When deeds came into use, the warranty was ex-

* See Grotius de Jure, 2. 9. 12.

† 5 Cruise, 84.

pressed. This would, of course, exclude any implied warranty inconsistent with the express; and in that sense it is true that *expressio unius exclusio alterius.* "For if A makes a feoffment by *dedi*, and in the deed doth warrant against J. S. and his heirs, yet *dedi* is a general warranty during the life of the feoffer," so that the feoffee could vouch the feoffer during his life. "And if a man make a lease for life, reserving a rent, and add an express warranty, here the express warranty doth not take away the warranty in law, for he hath the election to vouch by force of either of them."* In a previous passage, p. 290, Coke states: "Note that by the Civil Law every man is bound to warrant the thing that he selleth or conveyeth, albeit there be no express warranty; but the Common Law bindeth him not, unless there be a warranty either in deed or in law, for *caveat emptor.*" Neither doth the Civil Law bind him to warrant, unless there be a warranty express or implied. It bindeth him to warrant every thing he selleth, for instance, land; so does every conveyance at Common Law. These are feoffment, fine, exchange, partition. But Coke has overlooked, in the above passage, the difference between conveyances at Common Law, and those having their operation under the statute of uses, — a difference of which Mr. Fearne has made great use in his essay on Contingent Remainders. It is this, that conveyances under the statute of uses transfer only the right of the donor, whilst those at Common Law convey the right of the party, destroy contingent estates, and invest the donee with an absolute fee. It is in the former

* 2 Co. Litt. 298.

that express warranty is indispensable, and to them that the rule *caveat emptor* properly applies. So *caveat emptor* applies, for the same reason, to sales by official persons, as sheriffs and masters in chancery, whose deeds are not properly conveyances, but memorials of the execution of judgments and decrees. It is plain, therefore, that the Civil does not differ from the Common Law, but from that law concerning conveyances which has grown up under the statute of uses.

The rule of the Common Law is, that the heir is not bound unless named. The extent of his liability is determined by the value of the assets. It is important to distinguish between his liability and the extent of it. When his consent was necessary to alienation, no doubt he was named or joined. So, after deeds came into use, he was named or joined, and his liability was to make recompense in case of the eviction of the tenant. Now an heir cannot divest himself of that character, for he is born heir; and if, therefore, the rule that the heir, if named, was bound, was strictly enforced, his heirship would have been often highly detrimental. To correct this, a modification was introduced, which did not alter the nature of heirship, but limited his liability to the amount of assets. The modification is sometimes expressed thus,—that the heir is bound only as tenant of the lands.* But it will be seen that the question therein was, substantially, whether the heir should have the benefit of the modification of the rule, and be held liable only to the extent of assets. His liability as heir was conceded. The like modification

* 3 Rep. 12, Harbut's case.

prevails in case the heir is named in a bond of the ancestor. Then the heir, as in the former case, is responsible as heir, but his liability does not extend beyond assets.* In an action on the bond, he was sued in the debet and detinet, whilst an executor is sued only in the detinet. The latter was the representative of the deceased debtor, the heir was charged *as the debtor.*† And he could not plead that there is an executor who has assets; he must confess the action and show the certainty of assets.‡ For the obligation is a personal lien. Now the heir cannot be accounted the *debtor* in such case, where all the personalty goes to the executor, without admitting that he and the ancestor are one, independent of assets. And in all this, says Lord Chancellor Macclesfield, "the Common Law imitated the Civil Law." §

The Romans regarded heirship just as the Common Law does. Insolvency was with them a disgrace,— not only to the unfortunate debtor, but to his family. It was a powerful objection, in vulgar apprehension, to the claims of a candidate for office, that his father was a bankrupt. To prevent this disgrace, the common practice was to appoint a slave the heir. Where he died intestate, the prætorian law intervened and permitted the heir to renounce his right as heir, and to take the estate, as a *possessor bonorum*, or tenant, or bailee,—who then filed his inventory of the assets, by which both he and the creditors, unless they could show fraud, were bound. In fact, it was a plea of *riens per descent*,—or only a limited amount of them. But the character of heir was unchanged. The Com-

* 2 Co. Litt. 303.
† 2 Saunders, 7. *a*, note.
‡ 2 Co. Litt. 303.
§ 1 P. W. 776.

mon Law did not pass through these modifications, but adopted the rule as it existed in the Civil Law of the later times.

It may be added, that the characteristics of heirship enter also into the law of conditions. A warranty is a covenant for the benefit of the donee and his heirs, a condition *generally* for the benefit of the donor and his heirs. Neither of these can be assigned, at Common Law, to a third person, but both of them descend to heirs. No chose in action can be assigned to a third person. Is descent an assignment to a third person? No heir can take by purchase the interest that he might take by descent. Now the heir does take by descent, and that is not an assignment to a third person. The only explanation of this difficulty is, that the heir in apprehension of law is one with the ancestor, *hæres pars antecessoris*. Hence his land is attributed to the father, his rights are vindicated by the father, and upon the death of the latter, the heir is not a third person, but the same person, and therefore personally a debtor for the obligations of the father. The effect, therefore, of the rule in Shelley's case and of warranty is to maintain the unity of person and estate.

CHAPTER XI.

DIVERSITY OF RIGHTS.

THE law recognizes this division of rights: — 1. Those which spring from the relation of parties to a particular purpose, as the rights springing from commerce by partners, and those rights which relate to a particular property, as of joint tenants. 2. Those rights which are not connected with any particular purpose or estate, the rights of an individual. Between the rights of a society, partnership, or joint tenancy, and those of an individual, not a partner, joint tenant, or corporator, there is a broad and plain difference. But when we consider that the same individual has rights as such, and also, at the same time, as a corporator, or partner, or joint tenant, or citizen, it is extremely difficult to define accurately what, in judgment of law, are the rights of the associate and the rights of the individual. Thus, the difficulty is very great in the case of rights to land in which the rights of the individual and of the corporator are intimately blended. It may be said, in general terms, that as a corporator or joint tenant his rights are such as the law of the corporation or joint tenancy recognizes. But the individual right springs from the general right, and is only distinguishable from it when the individual exercises it. So that this general proposition, however true in the abstract, does not aid us in obtaining a clear apprehension of the cases to which it is properly applicable. Now, the necessity of some rule by which we may distinguish these classes of right is very manifest, for thereby in practice we should arrive at correct conclusions, not only as to the rights, powers, and duties of the corporator, but also of the individual. Such a rule, for example, would determine when a contract bound an individual as a partner, — that is, was obligatory on the partnership, — and when it did not bind that society, but bound the individual. It is plain that the question under consideration, therefore, touches the foundation of the most important affairs of corporations public and private, partnerships, and all other unions of men, with or without connection to property.

Perhaps the nearest approximation that can be made to certainty in the mode of distinguishing these classes is by reference, not to the nature of the right, *but to the exercise of the means of maintaining and preserving it.* For instance, the state protects each individual in the enjoyment of his property, without denying to him the right of protecting it himself. But it does not interfere and use the means of protection, unless the invasion of property is accompanied with disturbance of the public peace. The state, before it interferes, regards the end for which it was formed. In like manner a corporation, the legal entity, does not become a party to a suit where the rights of one corporator are invaded by another; nor where one partner injures his copartner, does the partnership interfere; and, in both these cases, for the reason that the end or purpose for which the society was created does not demand it. But in all these cases, where the end or purpose does require it, the corporation, partnership, joint tenancy, or other association, does become a party. There are cases, however, in which the corporation or state may interfere, without denying, at the same time, the right of suit to the individual, as in case of an assault and battery. But still the ends intended to be accomplished by the state and by the person injured are different. The former vindicates the public peace, the latter, the wrongs done to his person. But it is clear that the suit has no reference to the nature of the right, for the individual may be, or he may not be, a member of the state. At the same time, it is to be admitted that the rule suggested does not meet every case that can be conceived. Thus, two persons own jointly White-acre and one of them owns Black-acre, the adjoining parcel of land, and a question arises as to the true boundaries; — or suppose that a firm claims to be a creditor of one of its members; — in such cases a regard to the end does not direct us to the proper means of determining that question. The same proposition was submitted to Pomponius, that eminent Roman lawyer, whose opinions have been adopted into the Digest. He answered, as we do, that, before the question could be determined by law, the society must be dissolved.

The law has three distinct purposes: — 1. To maintain the existence and well-being of society. This is true of every society, public or private, corporate or incorporate. 2. To maintain and preserve the person and property of each individual member free from all burdens which are not common to every other member. 3. To maintain and preserve the special rights of each member, and also of each member in relation to property. These special rights of person are, for example, the rights of magistrates, — special rights of property, as easements. These manifestly are altogether accidental, varying in various societies and in the same society at various times, and always dependent upon the will of society. But the first and second class are fundamental principles, which cannot be varied in any material degree, without the destruction of the very purposes of society. We shall, therefore, omit all further notice of the third of these classes.

The means of accomplishing the just end are sometimes general and sometimes individual; — general, when a society defends itself or asserts its rights against non-members, or members; individual, when one member invokes the aid of the law against a fellow-member. As to the second class, the means are individual; — thus, an individual or class, upon whom a tax supposed to be unequal is imposed, or a larger share of contribution towards debts. But it is evident that in all such cases of the second class the party complaining must be a member. Hence an alien is excluded from participation in any thing relating to the society, — not because he lives under a different law, but because his existence is not recognized by the society. His condition is not exceptional, for the law as a unity has no exception, but many parts. So, likewise, and on the other hand, where the individual by any means ceases to be a member, his right as a member to exercise the means of preserving his person and property ceases.

It follows from the foregoing proposition, that society has no right to impose unequal burdens on any member, — that any member has a right to the means of preventing it. That, while every member is bound to the extent of his ability to maintain and preserve the society, his obligation is limited by reference to the ends of society. That, to accomplish these ends, he must have a voice in the management of affairs, — to be used for the preservation and well-being, and not the destruction, of society. That, sharing the burdens, he is enabled to participate in the benefits of society, and *vice versâ*. The parallel between a state and every other society might be still further extended. But sufficient has been said to illustrate the rule suggested.

Now these same principles are equally applicable, if we consider an individual of one state, in reference to a foreign state. Then the diversity of rights is a part of the *jus gentium.* For example, an American is acknowledged by every European power as having rights, not only if he happens to be within its territorial limits, but even although he may never have entered them. The *lex loci contractus* will always prevail, except in those few cases in which the public law of the state where the contract is sought to be enforced may forbid. This branch of the law may be accurately termed the private international law. It is apprehended that the common term *conflict of laws* is altogether misapplied. Dr. Story's work on the subject is not a treatise on the conflict of laws, but on the agreement of laws. Where the law of one state is in conflict with that of another, it depends entirely upon the forum which law will prevail. It is only necessary to refer to that learned work to establish this opinion. The diversity of rights between the American and the Frenchman exists only so far as the law of the corporation renders the latter the possessor of, and denies to the other, certain corporate privileges.

CHAPTER XII.

JOINT TENANCY.

This species of estate furnishes the most perfect instance of the principle of unity as applied to interests owned by two or more persons. It is one estate as to the state, as to the tenants, and as to third persons, being held by unity of time, title, interest, and possession. This unity can be destroyed at Common Law only by the voluntary act of the parties. Its relation to tenancy in common is identical with that of partnership to part-ownership, and it will be found, upon examination, that the principles of the former are generally applicable to joint tenancy. The *jus accrescendi* rests upon this idea, that each owns the whole estate,—*singulis in solidum debetur.** Such, too, is the rule of partnership. Coke states that an alien can take as a joint tenant, and that the state cannot interfere until the estate has vested in him by survivorship, for the other tenant owns the whole fee, *in solido*, as he expresses it.† It may be doubted whether this statement is correct. Undoubtedly the escheat cannot take place before survivorship, for the reason given; but if he were disseized by his cotenant, he would have been remediless. The enjoyment, therefore, of the usufruct would be altogether dependent upon the will of his cotenant. Moreover, by no manner of means could he acquire jurisdiction, for that is an attribute of the law, and the alien can take nothing by law, not even a usufruct for life. To admit him to be a joint tenant, in the legal signification of the term, would lead to the direct contradiction of some of the most certain rules of the law. He would have the right to bring a real action, to attend court as one of the *pares*, &c., &c.; in short, to exercise those rights which, by the Common Law, were peculiar to citizens. A very serious prac-

---

* G. Hugo, I. 407.

† I. 852, 786.

tical difficulty would impede even the joint tenant who is a citizen, if he was forced to bring ejectment. Can he sue alone? The production of his title-deed would prove that he had a cotenant; if he joined him in the action, he would fail by reason of the alienage. But if the court should regard him, as in theory he unquestionably ought to be, as non-existing, then the same result would follow as if he were dead, — the other would be sole owner. It was held by Lord Hardwicke, that where a legacy was left to two persons, in words that would make them joint tenants, if one of them died before the testator the whole passed *in solido* to the other, — not by survivorship, but by force of the words, which made him sole owner.* It is said that an alien may take, but cannot hold. Of course nothing more is meant than that, so long as the state does not interfere, he may enjoy the use and profits. The difference between him and a mere occupant without title is not very plain, for the latter may enjoy the use and profits until ejected by the party having the right. But neither the alien nor the tortious occupant can be said to have the right. Besides, the occupancy of the latter will finally ripen into right, whereas that of the former never can resist the claim of the state.

The idea of the *jus adcrescendi* is more correctly expressed in the phrase *jus non decrescendi*. "Dicitur etiam jus adcrescendi inter collegiatorios, et quod tamen magis est jus non decrescendi." † This is manifestly true, for in the case, by way of example, of a joint tenancy, the survivor does not take the other half of the fee by the death of his cotenant;

* 1 P. W. 700. † R. J. 123.

on the contrary, he had the whole during their joint lives, and it is not decreased by the death of the survivor.* They have not, one of them a seizin of one half, and the other of the remaining half, but each has an undivided moiety of the whole, not the whole of an undivided moiety. This is what causes joint tenancy to differ from substitutions and remainders. In the latter, the survivor takes that of which he had no seizin in the lifetime of the deceased. In the latter, one person is substituted in place of another; in the former the person is not changed. The rule being thus understood, and such clearly is its true meaning, it has a very extensive application in the law. Two joint tenants are *una persona*, and have *unicum patrimonium*, or one estate. So a corporation, a partnership, a family, a state, are each one person and possess one estate in apprehension of law. Death does not decrease nor increase the estate, nor destroy the civil person.

CHAPTER XIII.

JUS ACCRESCENDI.

To the citizen alone was the privilege accorded by the Twelve Tables of declaring the testamentary law of his estate. Sovereign over his family, his individual will was the public law of the family, and prevailed over that of the family, the law of nature. This is

* 2 Cruise, 487.

also one of the distinctive characteristics of the Common Law. In the former, the identity of the civil person of the ancestor and heir was rigorously observed, so that, in the language of Papinian, *una persona, unicum patrimonium.* Hence, *nemo potest pro parte testatus pro parte intestatus.* The testator named only one *persona* as heir, which, however, might comprehend several individuals, to whom his whole estate passed *per universitatem*, as an entirety. Now in case one of the individuals to whom the estate was devised deceased, the other took his share. Because the will of the testator, having in early times been a law made by an ancestor in the assembly of the people, with their consent, repealed, as to his family, the general law of succession, and of course repealed it altogether; so that, to obey this private law, no part of the estate could pass to his next of kin. The share of the deceased was transferred to the survivor, to preserve at once the unity of the estate and effect the will of the testator. "Jus accrescendi est quia nemo simul testatus et intestatus recte moriebatur Romæ." *

The Common Law has not adopted the rule that one cannot die partly testate and partly intestate, although it has received the *jus accrescendi.* The Civil Law maintained much more rigorously the unity of patrimony, and hence preferred the legatee to the heir by blood; whilst the Common Law favors the latter, or the diversity of patrimony. The Gallo-Romans knew nothing of testaments until the conquest by the Romans. There are, however, traces of a custom of transferring, in the lifetime of the testa-

* Bynkershoek, Obs., Lib. 2. c. 3.

tor, by way of sale, his property to a devisee, but limited to those cases in which the testator had no heirs of his body. The heir by blood was always preferred to the devisee, and a difference as to the classes of persons to whom they should descend was made between paternal and maternal inheritances. This was perfectly consistent with an exception to the rule, *Nemo potest pro parte testatus, &c.*, that had been introduced into the Civil Law by Cæsar, and perpetuated by Trajan, namely, that a soldier might die partly testate and partly intestate. After this time, the rule was thus propounded: "Nemo potest pro parte, testatus, pro parte intestatus decedere, nisi sit miles cujus sola voluntas in testando spectatur." The object of this rule was to enable the soldier to dispose of his "peculium castrense" to one person, whilst his other property passed either to another legatee of a will made in solemn form, or descended to his heirs by blood. The diversity of patrimony was in exact accordance with the Gallic customs, so that when wills began to be used the military will was selected. It became the fashion of making a testament, and was again transmitted to the German tribes; for, as is said by the learned Loysel, they *comme gens de guerre ont recu plusieurs patrimoines et divers heritiers d'une même personne.**

The Common Law has preserved the diversity of patrimony and the military will. But has also, as in all other instances, adopted the Civil Law rules of interpreting them. Hence, whilst the paternal and maternal inheritances descend to different heirs, yet, in reference to each class, the rule of *jus accrescendi*,

---

* Inst. Cout. Lib. 2. 5.

or the unity of estates, is adopted. Regarding each class in itself, the rule is, *Una persona, unicum patrimonium.*

CHAPTER XIV.

USUFRUCTS.

An estate for life is the lowest species of estate which requires livery of seizin. Littleton classes it with a term for years. "And the lessor is properly where a man letteth to another lands or tenements for term of life or for term of years, or to hold at will, he which maketh the lease is called lessor, and he to whom the lease is made is called lessee." * It was, however, regarded as a higher estate than terms for years, because the life estate conferred jurisdiction. A principality might be held for life, with dominion over its inhabitants. But in modern times, since the feudal system expired, and its traces in the law have been almost entirely obliterated from every portion of it, and altogether from estates for life, courts have regarded them merely according to their true nature. Setting aside all considerations as to jurisdiction, they have held that an estate for a number of years equal to those of human life was equivalent to a life estate. A term for life is only a term of years equal to the duration of life. Supposing that terms for years were granted during the feudal age, the want of livery of seizin rendered the title insecure; the contract and

---

* 2 Co. Litt. 719.

its execution wanted the ordinary publicity or evidence of its existence. They were at the will of the parties, and might be annulled at pleasure. Hence they fell under the denomination of "precaria"; but as society advanced, and writing came into use, they became contracts cognizable in courts, — whilst tenancy by sufferance and at will continued to be, as they are now, *precaria*. But even as early as the time of Fleta, that which was a tenancy at will, if verbal, was a term, if written; * and daily observation shows that these precarious interests are now ripening into terms for a year. Now we have seen that Littleton classes life interests with terms for years, and that the law regards them as only equivalent to a term of years. We apprehend, therefore, that life estates, as well as terms for years, are properly usufruct interests in contradistinction to proprietary. They form the highest in that class, whilst by their ancient attribute of jurisdiction they unite the usufructuary class with the proprietary. Now a usufruct interest is a bailment, — the relation of the parties that of letting and hiring, — and in reference to property it is a chattel. The tenant for life has the rights and the duties which Domat states to be pertinent to the bailee; he should put the thing to no other use than that for which it was hired, — he must commit no waste, — he must restore it at the time appointed, — do the service or pay the rent, — and, in general, observe whatever is required by law, custom, or the contract. On the other hand, he is entitled to the profits. The correctness of Littleton's classification, and the truth of our remarks, are shown in his seventy-first section.

---

* 1 Co. Litt. 735.

There he states that, "if a house be leased to hold at will, the lessee is not bound to sustain or repair the house as tenant for term of years is tied." "For," says Coke, "the statute of Gloucester extends not to a tenant at will, and therefore for permissive waste the lessor hath no remedy." * Now by that statute the lessor had an action for permissive waste against the lessee for life as well as for years. † So that at Common Law neither the tenant for life, years, nor at will, was bound to repair. That these were bailments appears from the concluding sentences of the section of Littleton above cited: "But if a tenant at will commit voluntary waste, as in pulling down houses, &c., the lessor shall have an action of trespass against the lessee. As if I lend to one my sheep to taothe his land, or my oxen to plough the land, and he killeth my cattle, I may well have an action of trespass against him, notwithstanding the *lending*." And the reason is, says Coke, that when the *bailee*, &c.

Now, it is apparent that a term of years, whether for life or for a certain number, is to that extent a diminution of the proprietor's usufruct interest in his estate. It is substantially a charge upon the principal estate, and, if no rent is paid, is of the nature of a *vivum vadium*. Every usufructuary interest is the use and enjoyment of the property of another. Now the difference between a right to a usufruct interest in another's land, for a term of years equal to the duration of a life, and a right to use a part of another's land as a way for the same period of time,— a right of way,—is only in the mode of enjoyment. Both are usufructs, and both are onerous on the es-

* I. 743. † I. 732.

tate of the proprietor. A right to an easement may, according to its nature, belong to one or more individuals, or to one or more by virtue of their connection with a particular tenement. In either case the easement is a charge upon the servient tenement, and a benefit to the parties enjoying it. Now the rights of the parties entitled to the easement and the duties of the party subject to it are identically those which we have seen pertain to the owner of a usufruct. The one is entitled to the full and free enjoyment of the easement without let or hindrance from the other, but he is not entitled to require the other, the bailer, or servient tenement, to repair. Thus the party entitled to a right of way cannot, in general, require the other to repair; if it becomes "foundrous," he must repair it himself or cease to use it, for he cannot go "extra vias," and travel over the adjoining land of the servient tenement,—no more than the tenants for life could require the proprietor to repair. The statute of Gloucester, however, has altered the Common Law so as to compel the tenant for life to repair, but the owner of a right of way has not yet been compelled by statute to do so likewise.

It is apparent, therefore, that the principles of the law which governs that extensive class of rights, the usufructuary,—including estates for life, for years, at will, and sufferance, and the multitudinous variety of servitudes,—are identically those of bailments. "I could not but observe with surprise," says Sir William Jones, in his preface to the Law of Bailments, "that a title which seems the most generally interesting should be the least understood and the least precisely ascertained. Hundreds and thousands of men pass through life without knowing, or caring to know, any of the numberless niceties which attend our abstruse though elegant system of real property, and without being acquainted with that exquisite logic on which our rules of special pleading are founded; but there is hardly a man who does not every day contract the obligations of a bailment; and what can be more absurd or dangerous than frequently to be bound by duties without knowing the nature or extent of them, and to enjoy rights of which we have no just idea?"

CHAPTER XV.

EXECUTORY INTERESTS.

Gradually, as the feudal law declined, uses and trusts advanced in importance. Jurisdiction was lost in the fee, and became undistinguishable from it. The courts began to regard estates in reference to usufruct rather than to that which is of much more public interest, power. Regarding the life estates, as they were amply justified in doing, when disconnected with jurisdiction, as a mere chattel interest, a term for ninety-nine years was held equipollent for the support of a remainder to a freehold. And on this view, that estates are only usufructs, is founded the whole doctrine of executory devises. "An executory devise is strictly," says Mr. Fearne, "such a limitation of a future estate or interest in lands or chattels as the law admits in the case of a will, though contrary to rules of limitation in conveyances at Common

Law." In a very early case it was held that a man might give a book (any chattel not consumed by use) to a person for his use during his life, and remainder over. Here, by distinguishing the usufruct from the legal property, a limitation directly contradictory of the rule of law was maintained. But no man can have in the nature of things more than a usufruct for life of any property or any power. The construction by which he has power over his estate after his death is not founded upon natural, but political reasons. It is the unity of jurisdiction that gives him the limitation to the heirs of his body, and declares that his heirs are so totally in him as a civil personage that he may give it to whom he will. Having, then, distinguished the usufruct from the legal estate, and thus avoided the rigor of the rule of law, all the canons of the doctrine of executory devises easily were deduced. Thus, as no man can have more than an enjoyment for life, if the use is limited to him and his heirs, and he dies, leaving no heirs living at the time of his death, there is no reason why another should not be named by the testator to succeed to the usufruct; or, as it is stated in the books, a fee may be limited after a fee. But it is proper to observe, that the use of the word *fee* either as expressive of jurisdiction or right at law is altogether erroneous; and, if taken in either sense strictly, would negative the existence of executory devises. Another corollary from the usufruct is, that an interest may be limited to commence *in futuro.* Commonly this is termed a freehold, but with a like disregard of correct language. It is not a freehold; which is a legal estate, but a chattel interest, and hence is consistent with the rule at Common Law by which a chattel interest may be made to commence *in futuro*. And lastly, because it is a chattel interest, it needs no particular estate to support it; whereas, if it were a freehold which required livery of seizin, it must have been preceded by a particular estate. There is another rule, that, where a limitation can be construed a remainder, it shall not be taken as an executory devise; that is, where the testator does not express his intention clearly that his successors shall be regarded as usufructuaries, the public law attributes jurisdiction to the estates created. The public law must prevail over the private law of any subject.

The misuse of the word *freehold*, in reference to usufructuary interests, has led to the difference of construction between the limitation of dying without issue, as applied to interests in lands and in chattels. It is admitted now that this difference is against grammatical construction, and the intention of the testator.* Hence the courts have resorted to other, and perhaps as doubtful, verbal criticisms to overcome or avoid former precedents. These are followed, where they are in point. It may be observed, that the whole discussion on the rule in Shelley's case between Mr. Fearne and Mr. Douglas depends on the difference of the legal estate from the usufruct. Their difference, too, was merely verbal, the one contending for the intention of the testator, the other for the rigorous enforcement of the rule at law. Had they agreed at first, that they were or were not disputing about a legal estate or a usufruct, the controversy could have proceeded no further. The true nature of the interest is manifestly the substance of the question. More-

---

* Fearne, 485, n. z.

over, by resolving the question into its true elements, we are enabled to place the decisions, often seemingly contradictory, upon a solid foundation, and to reconcile them. The general law must be observed, unless the private lawgiver, the testator, exercises his power to make an exception from it by his own will, in such a clear and unequivocal manner as excludes doubt. So, in like manner, where a person has a power granted by a deed, his exercise of that power must clearly and unequivocally refer to its source; and if it does not, it will either transfer only such interest as he possesses, or be utterly void. In short, the rule in Shelley's case must be enforced, unless the testator has otherwise directed; but the person affirming the exception to exist must prove it.

"The great and essential difference between the nature of a contingent remainder and that of an executory devise consists in this: that the first may be barred and destroyed, or prevented from taking effect by several different means; whereas it is a rule that an executory devise cannot be prevented or destroyed by any alteration whatsoever in the estate out of which or after which it is limited."* Certainly, when a limitation is admitted to be an executory devise, it cannot be barred; but that consequence of its nature does not, as Mr. Fearne states, explain its nature. It is a usufruct, the enjoyment of which depends upon a condition, and not a legal estate upon condition. A feoffment cannot operate except on strictly legal estates, and in such cases as might possibly have existed at the time when they were made in open court. As to usufructs, they are inapplicable, and when a

* Fearne, 418.

conveyance made in that form has been recognized as of any validity or effect, it has been as a *quasi* conveyance under the statute of uses. The great and essential difference, therefore, between contingent remainders and executory devises is, that the former are limitations of legal estates upon condition, and the latter are limitations of the usufruct upon condition. A usufruct is a bailment, and there is no rule of law or reason which forbids a contract for the creation of a bailment at a future period, without a precedent bailment in some one else ; nor that a party may not enjoy a bailment to the end of his life, and then that it shall pass to another, or several others, upon condition ; nor that another may not, on a certain event, participate with the bailee in the enjoyment of it. In short, upon this fundamental distinction between legal estates and usufructs depend all executory interests in lands or in chattels.

CHAPTER XVI.

POLITICAL STATUS.

Having traced the consequences in the law of real estate of the attribution to the landlord of sovereignty over his vassals or tenants, we are further to consider this principle in reference to personal rights. As has been before observed, no one in the feudal age, and therefore in the Common Law, held lands because he possessed political rights ; on the contrary, he possessed political rights only because he was a landlord.

Personal liberty existed, but the man who had no more was not the *liber homo* of Magna Charta. His condition was inferior to that of the landlord, and he stood in the middle, between the lord and the villain. In short, the non-landholder had no political *status;* he was not what we term a citizen. In the documents of the Middle Ages, citizens were known as *liberi homines*, *pares curiæ*, *legales homines*, and by various other titles, all of which meant that they were good men and true. These formed the basis of the whole organization, political, civil, and social, and included every citizen, whether king or subject.

The importance of this element of sovereignty — the *status civitatis* — has not been sufficiently developed, nor perhaps appreciated, by our juridical writers. Accurate digests of all the cases have been made, but neither their true reason nor the extensive ramifications of it seem to have been understood. This has arisen, probably, from the defective method in which they have treated of every portion of the Common Law. From Bracton, inclusive, they have in regular succession followed the arrangement of the Institutes of Justinian. In them, no notice is taken of the subject of citizenship, and for an adequate reason. By a series of laws, commencing at an early period of the Republic, the *status civitatis* was gradually bestowed upon the whole Roman world. An alien did not exist within its borders; therefore it was unnecessary for Justinian — in a work intended merely to teach the neophytes of the law-schools at Berytum, Constantinople, and Rome, the rudiments of the law as it then existed — to mention a subject only interesting to legal antiquarians. But it is far different in relation to the Common Law, and our writers have no excuse for their perfunctory method of treating of it. We will consider it first as it concerns the state, and then as it concerns the individual and the family, and the rights of property appertaining to these relations.

It is necessary, for the elucidation of this topic, to premise a few things. In these States, every man has a right to vote, and thus to participate in legislation, without regard to his possession of property. But under the old Common Law, the right to impose taxes was confined to those who had property to be taxed. It was against its fundamental policy to permit a person who did not share the burdens of taxation to impose them on his neighbors. Representation was inseparable from taxation, and taxation was always connected with representation. We use these phrases, familiar to us at present, to express the same principle that was contained in the phrase, the attribution of sovereignty to property. Again, it is to be also observed, that in every code of laws there are principles peculiar to that code, and others common to all civilized nations. For instance, the attribution of sovereignty to property was peculiar to our system; but the principles of the law of personalty are almost universal. It has been the practice adopted generally by nations, to confine the right to hold a part of their territory to citizens, and this has not been supposed to be detrimental to any of their important interests; whilst to extend that rule to personal property would manifestly cut them off from the society of nations. Now, the law of personal property is the law of nature, so far as it is cognizable in courts of justice. The Romans, and after them modern civilians, termed it the *jus gentium*, by which they meant that body of rules which are generally recognized by all civilized nations as obligatory upon *individuals.* It must not be confounded with the law of nations, or international law; nor, on the other hand, with that law of nature of which moralists treat. Touching the latter, it is to be observed that it is, as propounded by speculative writers, directly antagonistical to the Common Law. The latter maintains, as its fundamental principle, that property and its consequences, political power, are of positive institution. By it no man can affirm himself entitled either to property or power, except by the common consent of the state. The right to land does not spring from occupation, but from the grant of the state; nor has any man a right to possess a share of political power who has not previously obtained a share of its territory. These principles are, beyond doubt, inconsistent with the opinions most popular in this country. It is not our office to defend either side, and therefore we omit further notice of them. Blackstone has termed the law of nature the will of God. This may be admitted. Cicero had anticipated this view; for he declares that he will not argue with any man concerning the law, who denies the existence of God, and that he is the source of laws.* But the important question is, How is that will to be known? Those who think that human reason is the true test of that will, easily arrive at conclusions which justify disobedience to all human laws. Assuming a state of nature once to have existed, in which all men were equal and all things were in common, it has been without difficulty deduced that property is robbery. It is not a little remarkable

* De Leg. 1. 6.

that the preachers of the law of nature include the most hostile classes of writers, — the Christian and the Deist. But all of them fortify their speculations by citations from the writings of the Roman lawyers who flourished under the Empire. At that time political rights were not only theoretically, but practically, denied, and no man save the Emperor could assert a right to his life, liberty, or property. Yet these lawyers agreed in these two fundamental propositions: "Quod ad jus naturale attinet omnes homines æquales sunt." "Ratio civilis jura naturalia corrumpere nequit." Their connection with the law of nature and its fruits, the doctrines which vex modern European society, is very plain. How, then, is the law of nature to be discovered? Revelation has disclosed to man the will of his Maker as to his internal life as an individual. His will as to nations, it is apprehended, will be discovered in those laws which prevail among civilized nations in all ages. These are the moral facts demonstrating his providence as certainly as any physical facts. The one is the physical law of nature, the other the moral. And where human reason, by speculation, anticipates these results, it deserves applause, but it does not constitute the test of their truth. They exist and are laws, whether discovered or undiscovered.

CHAPTER XVII.

JUDICIAL OFFICE.

THE author of Fleta counsels the king, "Caveat sibi ne in sede judicandi quemquam loco suo substituat insipientem et indoctum, corruptibilem vel severum." * Can an alien sit in the seat of the sovereign? Whether sovereignty resides in one or many, sovereignty becomes subject by the delegation of jurisdiction to an alien power. The recognition by King John of the Pope as his feudal lord, which includes jurisdiction, was felt to be, and was resisted as, a violation of the fundamental law of the state. Indeed, such a doctrine never could have obtained the sanction of the descendants of the Norman conquerors. It is matter of history, that William took an oath to observe the native laws, but he committed the administration of them to his Normans, and speedily they were subverted. Jurisdiction could not, consistently with public safety nor the feudal law, be delegated to any but a member of the body politic. Certainly, before the separation of jurisdiction from property, no alien could have been a judge. That foreigners, in the troublous years that followed the death of the Conqueror, did occasionally occupy judicial places, is certain, but this was an incident of civil strife when laws were silent. Henry the First, in a capitulary, declared that "peregrina vero judicia, omnibus modis submovemus." Such is the law of the

* Lib. I. c. 17.

present day; five centuries have produced no change. The same is true also of every portion of the administration of justice. No alien can, by Common Law, be returned of juries for the trial of issues between the state and a subject, or between subject and subject. The jury *de medietate* is by statutory enactment. The objection that kings of England have been alien born, and have the power of appointing judges, is of no force; for the descent of the crown is *per se* an act of naturalization, and removes all the impurities from the fountain of justice.

CHAPTER XVIII.

COURTS.

Among the earliest changes in the feudal system was the creation of courts, in which the feudal lord did not exercise jurisdiction in person, but by means of his delegates. But this transference of jurisdiction made no change in the principles upon which it was exercised. It was less summary, more formal, and more just. A feudal lord had jurisdiction only over his own vassals, and his own land; without both were subject to him, he could not decide the controversy. When the trial of causes relating to land was assigned to the Court of Common Pleas, it also had jurisdiction only in case both vassals and land were within the territorial limits. Hence, as the lord could not try a cause concerning land in another domain, neither can that court an ejectment for lands in Ireland. Nor can it try a cause in which the king prosecutes a criminal, for that has been assigned to another court. Nor can the King's Bench try a land cause, nor a criminal whose offence has been committed out of the domain. In short, each court must possess competency as to persons and subject-matter, and all of them united possess all the jurisdiction that the feudal lord possessed. They are the delegates of the jurisdiction of the state. Hence, as they are delegates of the lord, they cannot derive jurisdiction from the consent of the litigants. They have it or have it not as delegates of the sovereign. Just as the vassal of one baron could not consent that his title to land in another baron's territory should be determined by the former. Under the feudal law, the recognition of the jurisdiction of another baronial court than that of which he was one of the *pares*, would have been punished by forfeiture, — for it was a denial of his allegiance. Sequestration to compel appearance and foreign attachment by custom are merely devices to compel an absent party to submit himself to the jurisdiction, and do not impinge on the principles already mentioned.

It was also a necessary consequence of the delegation of jurisdiction, that courts should so frame their modes of procedure as not to contradict the fundamental principle of their authority, competency as to jurisdiction and to property. It was not less necessary that this unity should exist in title to land, than in the court which was to determine a controversy concerning it. And this is equally true of all other courts, — civil, maritime, naval, and ecclesiastical. They must possess competency as to persons and subject-matter. The observance of this principle has been strict, and is discoverable in the least important matters of special pleadings. Thus, in a real action, the venue is said to be local, and must be stated to be within those territorial limits which the ancient Court Baron, whose jurisdiction the Common Pleas now exercises, formerly supervised. So, likewise, in personal actions, the venue, though transitory, — that is, may be alleged of any place, — must be of some place within the territorial limits of the court. Jurisdiction over the person and the subject-matter must be united. It is apparent, therefore, that the same principle of unity which forms the basis of the political and territorial organization of the state, forms also the foundation of all courts, — of their forms and rules of procedure. It concerns the greatest questions that can arise, without disregarding so petty a technicality as whether a venue shall be local or transitory. For the reasons already stated, the same controlling power is exercised by it over courts having the adjudication of crimes, and the imposition of forfeitures and punishments, — their proceedings and their forms.

The baronial courts never exercised what we term criminal jurisdiction. The distinction between public and private judges is found in the earliest period of the Middle Ages. Savigny has noticed the fact, that the compilations of laws made by the various conquering tribes were criminal codes, with a few provisions as to rights of property. They reserved to themselves, necessarily, the administration of public justice. Masters of the country by right of the sword, they had, even according to the Roman maxims, the criminal jurisdiction. The count, or by whatever other name the chief was called, recognized no distinction between his follower and his subject, as to crime, — both were equally under the power of the sword. Between them, as to offences, the difference was only in the degree of punishment. Hence it is that the public law of the feudal age differs altogether from the private, — not only in principle, but also in its forms of procedure. In the former there is not the slightest trace of Roman law, in the latter it is always discoverable.

CHAPTER XIX.

CITIZENSHIP.

It is evident from what has been said, that the citizen or landholder held, in relation to the non-landholder, a position of dignity and superiority. Savigny thinks that *dignity* is the proper word, and expresses accurately the idea of citizenship in the feudal age. "Thus there was one dignity common to all freemen, and a higher dignity confined to the nobility. The words *dignity* and *freeman* correspond to those of *caput* and *civis optimo jure* among the Romans."* He refers to the period of the Republic, when the patricians were distinguished from the plebeians rather by the antiquity of their origin than the importance of their privileges, and when the name of *civis* was common to all classes of citizens. This dignity was carefully protected from usurpation

---

* Hist. M. A., I. sec. 54.

by rendering it impossible for an alien to become a member of the community, except by obtaining the solemn and public consent of the sovereign, or state. This sentiment of the dignity of citizenship was, as we have seen, a striking trait in the character of the Germans, as well as of the Romans. The lord and the vassal, the noble and the plebeian, were equally proud of it. We have three remarkable historical instances in proof of this assertion. A barbarian, half naked and possessed of only the rudest arms, haughtily told Cæsar, "Liberum se, liberæque civitatis." * The Apostle Paul, born of the despised race of conquered Judea, when about to be scourged by a centurion, said, "I am a Roman citizen," and "the chief captain went away afraid." A Roman Senator, Scipio, the second Africanus, being interrupted in the midst of a speech by the murmurs of a crowd of adopted citizens who stood around the tribune, struck them mute with the insolent exclamation, "Silence! ye bastards of Italy." The barbarian, the Christian Apostle, and the pagan Senator equally felt proud because they "had inherited the ennobling quality of original citizenship." We have quoted the words of a German who himself felt this sentiment, and who of all men that have lived in modern times best understood the character and history of Rome, — Niebuhr. †

This common sentiment of the dignity of the citizen led among the German tribes, when they became landholders, to the establishment of rules for the protection of this dignity identical with those used by the Romans. Thus the slightest infringement upon

---

* Comm. 5. 7, and 3. 10.

† Vol. I. p. 238.

his land was a great wrong; it was a trespass, although the trespasser had merely walked over uninclosed land. His house was his castle, and upon no pretence could be entered without his consent, unless the highest public interests required it. It was his castle, because, say Lord Coke and Gaius, "domus tutissimum cuique refugium atque receptaculum." * His person was sacred, and he might put his assailant to death in case his own life was in peril. Such, also, is the rule of the Civil Law as stated by Gaius.† A burglar might be put to death *si nox furtum factum est, si eum aliquis occidisset jure cæsus esto.* A robber of a dwelling-house by day shall be beaten with rods, — *si luci furtum faxit.* A robber by day, if armed and he defends himself, may be killed, provided the assailed cries for help, — *si se telo defenset, quiritato, plorato que, post deinde,* &c. ‡ In the early age of the Republic the creditor had what Lord Coke calls a personal lien, — *nexus,* — a mortgage of the person of the debtor, — and might, upon his default in payment, have kept him as his slave or sold him. The gambling debts of the Germans were frequently paid in the same manner. The Common Law has adopted the modification of the rule which was introduced in the time of Theodosius, by whom it was declared that imprisonment of a debtor for the smallest space of time was a full satisfaction: — "Nec sane remuneratione precii debet exposcere cui, etiam minimi temporis spatio servitium satisfecit ingenui." §

The dignity of the baron, the citizen, protected

* Semayne's Case.

† Lib. 1.

‡ Twelve Tables.

§ Cod. Theod. III. 3. 1.

his family; a word including his estate as well as his wife, children, and dependants. Hence, to do an injury to his wife, either in person or character, or to his children, or to his servants, was *his* wrong. They, and their earnings and acquisitions, were his, and they could be vindicated only by him. Except through him, they had no rights of which the law took notice. The jurisdiction over his vassals was exercised by virtue of their possession of parts of his domain; but over his wife, children, and servants, because they were part of himself.

CHAPTER XX.

ALIENS.

It is commonly said that an alien has capacity to take a fee simple by purchase, but not to hold it; and that he cannot even take by an act of law. The proposition would be more accurately stated thus: that by the Common Law lands can be holden only by citizens. It is not sufficient that the person be innocent of crime, or have paid the full value to the owner; he must also have the *status*. Nor is the exclusion of the alien a penalty upon the person for being born out of the ligeance; nor after he has purchased is the escheat in the nature of a forfeiture.* On the contrary, in the judgment of law, the alien, so far as the holding of lands is concerned, does not

---

* 2 Brown, P. C. 91.

exist, and the escheat takes place as if the last owner had deceased without heirs. It is indispensable that the person should be a member of the political community, free of the corporation, in order to enjoy any of its benefits. That land is holden only in virtue of political character is shown conclusively by the fact, that a native is not necessarily entitled to purchase and hold it. As where a villain, who in the Common Law is called *nativus*, "purchases in fee simple or in fee tail, the lord of the villain may enter into the land and oust the villain and his heirs for ever; and after, the lord may, if he will, let the same land to the villain to hold in villainage." * So, where a freeman held lands by villainage, he had no political rights, — did not participate in the administration of justice by courts, — and differed in no respect from a villain. On the other hand, a villain who purchased lands, and held them by a free tenure, was, except as to the lord, a freeman. The villain, by manumission of his lord, became a citizen, as the alien does by naturalization. In both cases they acquire *status* on the same principle, — adoption into the political family. This appears from the comments of Lord Coke upon the word *enfranchisement:* "It is derived from the word *franchise*, that is, liberty, and in the Common Law hath divers significations; sometimes incorporating of a man to be free of a company or body politic; sometimes to make an alien a citizen, and here to manumise a villain or bondman." † The alien must receive the franchise of membership of the body politic. This could be obtained only with the consent of the sovereignty;

* 1 Co. Litt. 405.

† Ibid. 497.

that for the villain was his lord, — for the alien, the state. A native freeborn man has now by the Common Law the common consent of all the members of the body politic, — the *status* as his birthright.

To hold lands, therefore, the person must be capable as well by the political part as by the *jus gentium* of the municipal law. By the former he participates in theory in the administration of the affairs of the state. It is the union of jurisdiction and property which constitutes a perfect title to land. In the case of the alien these are severed, and hence he has no voice in the formation or administration of the law. He is not one of the *pares curiæ*, and therefore cannot institute an action real or mixed; but having the benefit of the *jus gentium*, he may institute a personal action. But even this was denied him in the early age of the Common Law. The foreigners who visited England were generally merchants, and most of them Jews, and were safe neither in life, liberty, nor property. The thirtieth chapter of Magna Charta, it is believed, is the first statutory enactment by which alien merchants obtained "salvum et securum conductum exire de Anglia, et venire, et morari et ire, tam per terram, quam per aquam," to buy and to sell. It is printed in all the editions of the statutes as of the ninth year of Henry III., but it is in fact a transcript from the roll of 25 Edward I., who at that time confirmed it. As late, therefore, as Edward I., none but merchants could visit England with safety. Other aliens, unless protected by a royal license, so far from acquiring lands and becoming feudal lords, entered the kingdom at the peril of their lives. No Habeas Corpus existed to release them from the dungeons of the noble outlaw. Thus more than two centuries after the Conquest* aliens were treated as enemies. The only modification of the rigor of this rule that has yet been made, is the permission of the alien to enjoy a lease of a house for habitation. This, too, is a judicial inference from the above-cited chapter of Magna Charta. So that, with this slight amelioration of his condition, the alien as to lands is as much under the ban of the law as when William the Conqueror enacted that "omnes liberi homines" should swear to defend his "terras et honores contra inimicos et alienigenos." In all ages of the Common Law, therefore, only citizens have had the capacity for the full enjoyment of all rights, political and civil.

CHAPTER XXI.

GUARDIANSHIP.

THE consequences of political *status*, as to the public and private rights of the individual, having been noticed, it is now to be considered in reference to the family. Nations have differed greatly in their laws as to paternal authority, but the feudal law recognized the relation between the father and his child only for political purposes. The father could not sell him into slavery, nor put him to death, nor control his conduct when he became able to do military service. As the heir apparent, he was treated with def-

---

* A. D. 1297.

erence by his father's retainers, but he was still only the first of his vassals. It was as a vassal that he was known to the law. The duties of the lord to the vassal were to protect him in his person and estate. When the vassal, from any cause, could not render the services due, the lord might enter upon his lands and take the profits, either temporarily or perpetually; the right was suspended or determined. Temporary suspension by reason of the infancy of the vassal was wardship. Now it is manifest that the lord — king or noble — held towards his minor vassal a paternal relation. Guardianship, which by nature belongs to the father, by the feudal law belonged to the lord. The latter was entitled of right to the care of the person as well as of the estate of his young vassal. The person and estate, property and sovereignty, were inseparable, except in those instances in which the vassal held lands of several lords. In such case possession of the person gave priority of right to its care and control. Thus the lord had over him *paterna potestas*, and was within his domain *parens patriæ*. This power controlled his nurture, — directed his education, his marriage, — and thus, in a great measure, determined the course of his life. It is evident that, if an alien was the father, the law denied him every right that the law of nature confers upon paternity. Over the estate of his child he could have no authority, nor, as a consequence, over his person. The family relations, therefore, depended for their existence upon the approval of the public law. All human ties were as non-existent, whenever they came in conflict with the principle of unity of sovereignty and property.

CHAPTER XXII.

COURTESY.

The guardianship of the wife by her husband necessarily gave him the management of her estate, and the enjoyment of its profits. It is only in an old and highly refined state of civilization that we discover traces of separate estates. The tenancy by courtesy unites, to a certain extent, guardianship and the institution of separate estate. This custom is said to have been introduced into England in the reign of Henry the First. This is extremely improbable, for the custom was well known in Normandy before the Conquest, and was too favorable to the husband to have fallen into desuetude. It may be that during that reign it first received judicial sanction; an opinion to which we incline, inasmuch as the cases referred to by our juridical writers are of a little later date. Traces of this custom may be found in the writings of the early portion of the Middle Ages. The Capitularies of Dagobert I. (A. D. 630) expressly mention it: "Si quæ mulier quæ hæreditatem paternam habet post nuptum prægnans peperit filium, et in ipsa hora mortua fuerit, et infans vivus remanerit aliquanto spatio vel unius horæ, hæreditas materna ad patrem pertinet," &c. The same passage is found also in the Code of the *Alemanorum*,* which, according to Savigny, was copied from the Bavarian.† A capitulary was rarely limited to a single tribe, but

* Lib. Al. 63.

† I. c. 9, s. 33. 4.

usually extended to the whole people, and it is highly probable, therefore, that courtesy was generally prevalent.

According to this passage courtesy was only of the lands which the woman derived from her father by descent. This is the interpretation given to *hæreditas* by Cicero: "Hæreditas est pecunia quæ morte alicujus ad quempiam pervenit *jure* nec ea aut legata testamento aut possessione retenta." Inheritance, in short, is by descent. In like manner a Roman magistrate presiding in Gaul, in the fourth century, writes to his legal friends in Rome this surprising fact, *Gignantur hæredes et non scribuntur.* This definition of Cicero is also implied in the Common Law rule that heirs take by descent, — *jure*, — for where they may take as heirs, they cannot take by purchase. The right by act of law — *jure* — is always higher than that by act of the parties. After the time of Cicero, *hæreditas* received a wider signification, and meant inheritance acquired by devise as well as by descent. "Ac prius de hæreditatibus despiciamus, quarum duplex condicio est; nam vel ex testamento vel ab intestato ad nos pertinent." *

Courtesy is also mentioned, as we have observed, in the Bavarian Code, which was compiled A. D. 637. Savigny states that, in a multitude of passages, the imitation of the Roman law is evident, although the particular texts which have been followed cannot be indicated. He remarks, however, on the passage from the Bavarian Code, (which contains the custom of courtesy, and also refers to a provision for the wife after the death of the husband,) that he recognizes in

---

* Gaius, 2. 99.

it two laws of Justinian, which grant to the survivor of the husband and wife an equal provision out of the profits of the estate of the other, and he cites these laws. But he observes also, that, while the law of Justinian allows this provision only in case the survivor is poor, the Bavarian Code takes no notice of this circumstance.*

It is not surprising, therefore, that courtesy should be found in the compilation known as the *Petri Exceptiones Legum Romanorum.* This work is supposed to have been written in the latter part of the tenth century (950 - 1000 A. D.). It contains a systematic exposition of the law as it then existed, and in a great degree of the Roman law. These are the words of chapter 33: "Si quis duxerit uxorem et dotem ab ea acceperit vivente uxore habeat omnes fructus dotis propter onera matrimonii. Ea vero defuncta siquidem nullos ex ea habuerit liberos, integro jure, &c. Si autem ex ea filios habuerit solum usum fructum habeat — liberi — autem proprietatem." Here, not only is the right of the husband to the enjoyment of the profits determined, but the distinction between the usufructuary and proprietary interests is expressly marked. It is noticeable, also, that Justinian allowed courtesy on account of the poverty of the husband; the Bavarian Code takes no notice of that fact, and the Petri Exceptiones gives the reason of the allowance of courtesy, *propter onera matrimonii.*

Glanville, it is to be supposed, knew the latter work, for he published his treatise A. D. 1186. Yet he states that courtesy was confined to the *maritagium*, which is synonymous with *dos*, and in this re-

* Vol. II. 55, s. 30.

spect is the same as the phrase *paternam hæreditatem* in our citation from the Capitulary. Now *maritagium* in the old Common Law books meant only "the lands which the wife bringeth in frank marriage." But it is not probable that Glanville used it in that limited sense, unless we suppose that he, the chief justice of a Norman prince, was ignorant of the laws and customs of the Normans. If it was first introduced into England by Henry, he derived it from Normandy, and during his reign Glanville wrote. We suppose, therefore, that Glanville used the word *maritagium* in a sense comprehending all the lands of the wife. The *Ancien Coutumier* * of Normandy allows courtesy in all the lands of the wife — *toute la terre* — of which she was seized at the time of her death. It is probable, however, that this contracted meaning of the word *maritagium*, as well as the notion that the husband could not be entitled unless he was poor, — a lackland, — did find acceptance among the civilians of that age. We say *civilians*, for the latter idea was to be found in none of the customary codes, but was mentioned by Justinian, and only by him. To cor-

---

* Our references to this code are taken from the learned work of M. David Houard, a distinguished lawyer of Normandy, entitled, "Anciennes Loix des François conservées dans les Coutumes Angloises, recueillies par Littleton." Rouen, A. D. 1766. It contains the Tenure of Littleton in Norman-French, accompanied by the Ancien Coutumier of Normandy. Its object, as the title of the work indicates, is to show that the ancient Norman customs are sources of the laws of England. No one who reads the work can doubt this fact; indeed, it has never been denied by any who have taken the pains to compare the Tenures with the Ancien Coutumier. We do not except Mr. Reeves, notwithstanding his remarks, Vol. II. p. 283, notes. At the same time, it must be allowed that the value of M. Houard's work consists in the amendment of the mutilated texts of Littleton, Glanville, Fleta, Britton, and the Mirroir, together with his collection of the Tenures and the Coutumier. Littleton copied verbatim and largely from the latter.

rect these errors, Bracton enters into details otherwise unnecessary. He propounds the rule thus, — that the husband, whether he had or had not an estate, was entitled to courtesy if he married a wife having "hæreditatem, maritagium, vel aliquam terram ex *causa donationis*." * Adding to this summary the word *dotem* (which is, however, synonymous with *maritagium* and therefore unnecessary to the sense), we have in this passage an epitome of the three citations that we have made.

Further, the Capitulary recognizes the distinction between paternal and maternal inheritances. By the Common Law if a man marries an inheritrix of lands in fee simple, who has issue a son, and the son enters as heir to the mother and then dies without issue, the heirs of the mother shall inherit, and not those of the father, for *paterna paternis, materna maternis*.† Then, in the example of courtesy put by Littleton, upon the death of the wife and the issue, the lands ought immediately to have descended to the heirs according to the rule *materna maternis*. But, on the contrary, it is disregarded and an exception made in favor of the husband by courtesy *propter onera matrimonii*. The use of the word *courtesy* in the sense of a rule of law is not peculiar to black letter; thus, "The courtesy of nations allows you my better, in that you are the first-born." ‡ When the reason ceased, where there was no issue, then the national sentiment, *Dotem non uxor marito*, concurred with the interests of the maternal heirs in enforcing an observance of the general rule of descent, *materna maternis*.

---

* Fol. 437.

† 2 Co. Litt. 178.

‡ Shakspeare, "As you like it," Act I. Sc. 1.

Such, then, is the origin of this doctrine, and the reason that tenancy by courtesy, to the requisites of its corresponding estate, dower, — namely, marriage, seizin, and death, — adds that of issue. As it does not differ from dower in reference to jurisdiction, we shall postpone our remarks on that topic to the chapter on Dower.

CHAPTER XXIII.

DOWER.

THERE are four kinds of dower at Common Law mentioned in our books. The dower *de la plus belle* could be obtained only by the judgment of a court, and its purpose was to prevent the division of lands which were subject as a unit to military service. In like manner, there cannot be partition or endowment of a castle held *pro defensione regni.**

Dower *ad ostium ecclesiæ* is in fact a jointure, which after the death of the husband the wife may refuse, and be endowed at Common Law. Coke observes that it could be granted only at the door of the church, because in this and like matters the law requires publicity and solemnity. So in the early ages of the Common Law all feoffments were made in the presence of the *pares curiæ.* Deeds executed by the parties were altogether unknown, for few of the priests, and fewer of the lords, could sign their names.

---

* 1 Co. Litt: 797.

But as the transfer was made in the presence of the vicinage, it had, as in cases of dowment *ad ostium*, all necessary publicity and solemnity. To perpetuate the proof of these contracts, it was customary to make a memorial of them in the chartulary or leger-book of some adjacent monastery.* Dowment made at the door of the church, under the patronage of the guardian saint, was in all probability duly entered in like manner by the priests. Mr. Turner has published such a memorial or marriage settlement in his valuable History of the Anglo-Saxons.† This kind of dower was also known in Normandy.

Dower *ex assensu* differs altogether from dower at Common Law. It is not assigned out of the husband's lands and tenements, but out of the father's or brother's; and the right to it is by act of the parties, and not by act of law. It is, like the *ad ostium*, a jointure, and must be created by deed. From the fact that a deed is indispensable, it is certain that it must be of comparatively late introduction into England. All the authorities cited by Coke are of the age of Bracton, about two hundred years after the Conquest, and as that was the most flourishing period of the Civil Law in England, it may also be inferred to owe its origin to that system. This species was well known to the Lombards, under the name of *faderfium*. The words of the Lex Rotharis, as cited by M. la Ferrière, are these: "De faderfio autem id est, de alio dono quantum pater aut frater dederit ei quando ad maritum ambulaverit."‡ A. D. 643. The Franks also used this species of dower. Marculf, a

* 2 Bl. Com. 342.

† Vol. II. p. 82.

‡ Vol. II. p. 158, n. 11.

Frank, and a monk of the diocese of Paris, compiled in A. D. 660 a book of forms. Among them is the precedent of a deed to create dower *ex assensu*, — *libellus dotis*.* Savigny refers to this work as a "most precious compilation," containing indisputable evidence of the wide-spread influence of the Civil Law in the Middle Ages. On the other hand, all the Common Law writers on the ancient feudal tenures cite his formula as authority.

The Petri Exceptiones mention it under the name of *propter nuptias donatio*. Chap. 7: "Si pater filiis in potestate constitutis donaverit, non valet donatio quam filio nurui præstat." Chap. 33: "Propter nuptias vero donatio, defuncta uxore, in patrimonio mariti revertitur, et inter alios res ejus computatur." † The Ancien Coutumier of Normandy also contains the same law. Civilians are agreed that the ante-Justinian law prevailed during the Middle Ages, and that the compilations of Justinian were unknown. The changes, therefore, which were made in the character of the *propter nuptias donatio* did not affect the Gallo-Roman provinces. This *donatio*, says Muhlenbruch, existed originally *apud orientes*, and was introduced into the Roman law by Constantine, A. D. 319. ‡ From Rome it passed to the provinces, and was adopted by the German conquerors. Their works of mixed law have transmitted it to us.

---

* Form. 2. 15. 6.

† 4 Savigny, App. No. 2.

‡ Muhlenb. W. P., Vol. II. sec. 539.

CHAPTER XXIV.

DOWER AT COMMON LAW.

TACITUS states that the custom of the Germans was, that the husband endowed the wife; and in this respect they differed from the Gauls, who required mutuality of gifts, and from the Romans, who united the Gallic custom with that of the wife endowing the husband. But it must not be supposed that Tacitus, in the sentence often cited by our juridical writers, — "dotem non uxor marito, sed uxori maritus," — referred to dower at Common Law. For in the next sentence he states that the parents or friends of the wife were always present to give their approval of the presents: "Intersunt parentes et propinqui ac munera probant." * It was, in fact, a jointure, and if not satisfactory, the marriage did not take place. Dower was known to them, however, under the name of *morgengabe*, and to the Saxons as *morgengift*, — both words meaning the gift of the morning after the marriage.† The consummation of the marriage evidently was necessary, and our Common Law writers plainly state that it was the "præmium pudoris." ‡ The Ancien Coutumier also gives the same reason; *au coucher gagne la femme son donaire.* The dower of the wife differed in quantity among the tribes, but the Franks, Burgundians, and Saxons allowed her one third part *de omni re quam simul collaboraverunt*, —

* De Mor. Ger. 23.

† 2 Turner, Ang. Sax. 85.

‡ 1 Co. Litt. 568.

de eo quod vir et mulier simul conquieverint. It was originally the wife's share of the land which she and her husband had jointly labored for or conquered. Now the Germans in their military emigrations were always accompanied by their wives, and their settlements were made, not as soldiers, but as tribes. As long as the husband and wife lived, they enjoyed together, to use the energetic expression of the Saxon law, their common conquest. Not only do their compilations of laws prove that this custom arose after their invasion of the Roman provinces, but it could not have arisen before; for, as they had no private estates in land, there could be no dower. Indeed, their first appearance on the banks of the Rhine was as fugitives seeking escape from more powerful tribes.* When, finally, they broke into the provinces, it was still by compulsion, being driven onwards by adverse fortunes in the wars which seem always to have vexed the regions whence they came.

The Normans seized upon a portion of France in the ninth century, about four hundred years after the first invasion of the German tribes. They adopted the customs of the Franks in a great measure, and allowed the wife one third as her dower. Littleton, in his thirty-sixth section, has copied almost *verbatim* the Ancien Coutumier: "Coutume est que la feme qui a son mari mort, ait la tierce partie du fief au temps qu'il epousa."

All the tribes condemned marriage with an alien. In A. D. 370, the Emperors Valentinian and Valens prohibited, under the penalty of death, the marriage of citizens and barbarians. The rigor of this law was

* A. D. 370, 406.

afterwards so modified as to permit such marriages with royal license. At length, however, Alaric became king of the Visigoths, and, assuming to himself and his barbarians the name of Roman citizens, revived the law in all its severity. His code declares that a lawful marriage can be contracted only between Roman citizens; — "Legitimæ sunt nuptiæ, si Romanus Romanam," etc.* Again, a Roman citizen cannot be in the power, as a ward, for instance, of *homo peregrinæ conditionis*.† Indeed, the Breviarium only expresses the universal sentiment and custom of the tribes. The full force of this prohibition can only be estimated by considering that in that age, and long afterwards, the conquerors and the conquered had not amalgamated. They lived in the same villages, upon adjoining farms; met daily and traded together; were mutually indebted for the various services of civility and humanity that contiguity produces; but marriage was impossible.‡ A want of *status*, whether by reason of alienage or bondage, rendered marriage infamous.

CHAPTER XXV.

MARRIAGE.

If a man seized of a fee in lands taketh an alien to wife and dieth, she shall not be endowed. Marriage, therefore, does not communicate to an alien woman

---

* Epit. Gaii, Lib. I. tit. 4.

† Tit. 6. sec. 1.

‡ 1 Savigny, ch. 3.

all the rights that it does to a native freeborn woman. Now Coke states that the only three requisites to entitle a woman to dower are marriage, seizin, and death of the husband; yet though the alien woman is married, and her husband hath seizin and dies, she shall not be endowed. It is clear, then, that the marriage meant is that between citizens. That there is an important difference between the marriage of citizens and that of a citizen and alien is made very manifest by this: that if a marriage be avoidable by divorce in respect of consanguinity, yet if the husband die before divorce, the wife shall be endowed; for this is *legitimum matrimonium, quoad dotem.** Here we see that an incestuous union, if not annulled in the lifetime of the husband, is a legitimate marriage *de facto*, — not *de jure*, as to dower. But *quoad dotem*, the alien woman did not contract even a marriage *de facto*. In England divorce is exclusively within the jurisdiction of the ecclesiastical courts, and in the case above stated the death of the husband prevented a sentence of divorce, — death had anticipated ecclesiastical censure. Hence the judge returns a certificate of *legitimum matrimonium*. But the death of the husband absolutely debars the alien wife from her claim of dower.

Bracton mentions the *justum et legitimum matrimonium*,† but does not explain or define it. Indeed, our juridical writers afford us no assistance. However, marriages, as we have seen by the citation from Coke, may be *de facto* or *de jure*, and of course there is a difference between them. In both cases the parties must be able, — willing and do consent.

---

* 1 Co. Litt. 658.

† Lib. 1. fol. 6.

These may be termed the requisites of the *jus gentium*. Our system adds that of citizenship in every contract relating to land. It is evident, then, that the *legitimum matrimonium* cannot be contracted *de facto* or *de jure* by an alien. For marriage in either case would have conferred upon her a full participation in all the rights of the husband. That such was the result of a legitimate marriage appears from the definition of it in the canonical law: "Viri et mulieris conjunctio, individuam vitæ consuetudinem, cum divini et humani juris communicatione, continens." *

Furthermore, it is to be considered that, in the earlier ages of the Common Law, land was almost the only species of property. To deny to the alien wife, therefore, any share of it, was a practical denial of all rights of property. Yet this was done by a system which recognizes the right to dower as not only a legal and equitable, but also a moral right.† So that the law did not recognize her existence at all in any civil or moral capacity. Moreover, dower was avowedly allowed *propter onera matrimonii et ad sustentationem uxoris*, — *de facto* or *de jure*. She, therefore, who was not entitled to it was not a wife.

It is to be observed that although aliens, male or female, have the capacity by the *jus gentium* to acquire lands, they are prevented by defect of political *status*. Being subject to the former, they may by descent or purchase acquire that kind of property regulated by that law, personalty. Here, again, we recognize the principle of unity and the correspondence of persons and property.

The *legitimum matrimonium* of the Common Law

---

* 4 Reeves, 52. † 2 P. W. 701.

is identical with the *connubium* of the Civil. That could not take place between slaves, — nor a slave and free person, — nor, except by license, between the alien and a citizen.* Such, too, is the Common Law in regard to the first two instances. And as to the last, we learn that, by a special act of Parliament, all women aliens who from thenceforth should be married to Englishmen by license of the king might demand dower.† *Connubium* was also termed *justum aut legitimum matrimonium*, — *justæ nuptiæ*, — in contradistinction to *contubernium*. The latter was not regarded as mere concubinage. It differed from *connubium* in this respect, that it conferred upon the wife no political equality with the husband, nor any participation in his religious observances or civil rights. On the other hand, *connubium* is exactly defined by the canonical definition of marriage. It was peculiar to citizens. "Connubium inter cives; inter civem autem et peregrinæ conditionis hominem aut servilis non est connubium sed contubernium." ‡ The maxim of the Common Law, "Consensus non concubitus facit matrimonium," was received as true only in reference to this species of marriage. § But under the influence of Christianity, although the distinction between the civil contract and the sacrament was not entirely obliterated, the Church considered consent as marriage between an alien and a citizen.

As the *connubium* was peculiar to citizens, so was the marriage ceremony of a corresponding character. There were three kinds of nuptial ceremonies, and two

---

* Fuss. Rom. A. Sec. 82.

† 1 Co. Litt. 661, note 15.

‡ Gaius, 1. 67.

§ Cod. Theod. III. 16. 1; 2 Comm. Code Alaric.

of them, *usus* and *confarreatio*, have some resemblance or analogy to the practices of modern times. The *usus* was where the wife domiciled with her husband for the space of a year, without being absent for three nights. The other, *confarreatio*, was the most solemn. The marriage was contracted in the presence of the father or guardian and of witnesses, before the altar, and accompanied with a sacrifice by a priest. By this form the wife became subject to the power of her husband, *in manum veniebat.** Hence the rule that he acquires the property of the wife,—"quam in manum ut uxorem receperimus, ejus res ad nos transeunt." Its coincidence in form and consequences with our mode of contracting lawful marriage is remarkable. In the early times of the republic all citizens and priests used it alone. When, however, Grecian manners had corrupted Rome, this, with many other ancient customs that had, fortunately for us, previously been adopted by the Germans, fell into desuetude.

We apprehend, therefore, that an alien woman could not contract with a citizen *justum et legitimum matrimonium* either by the Civil or Common Law. Nor, indeed, by the canonical law, unless we suppose that, by the phrase *humani juris*, only natural law is intended. That may be the correct view, as it is derived from the Justinian law, and in his age citizenship and humanity were coincident. The *jus gentium* was the law of the Empire.

---

* Gaius, 2. 98, 109.

CHAPTER XXVI.

CONVEYANCES.

THERE existed in the feudal law, as we have seen, a correspondence of persons and property, the result of the attribution of sovereignty to the landed proprietor. The Germans, says Savigny,* had a species of perfect property like the *dominium ex jure quiritium* of the Romans. Of course he means that in the Middle Ages, after their conquests, they had such property, for before that time, as has been frequently observed, they had no private estates in land. It could be held only by citizens. "Aut enim ex jure quiritium unusquisque dominus erat aut non intelligebatur dominus." The ennobling quality of citizenship was his right to hold it. It is not surprising, therefore, that citizens should have peculiar modes of transferring this perfect property. The Common Law had only three original kinds of conveyance, — feoffment, exchange, and partition. Exchange is, in fact, two conveyances, and might therefore be properly removed from the class of original conveyances. Our remarks on the subject of feoffment are equally applicable to exchange.

Feoffment was known to the Romans and Gallo-Romans under the name of *cessio in jure*. The latter was employed to transfer, not only lands and things savoring of realty, but also slaves. Gaius gives the most precise directions for the mode in

---

* I. 134.

which it should be made. "In jure cessio hoc modo fit; apud magistratum populi Romani velut Prætorem vel apud præsidem provinciæ is cui res in jure ceditur rem tenens ita dicit. Hunc ego (hominem, fundum) ex jure quiritium meum aio,—deinde postquam hic vindicaverit, prætor interrogat eum qui cedit an contra vindicet. Quo negante aut tacente tunc ei qui vindicaverit, eam rem addicit." This is the exact method in which a feoffment at Common Law was made. It was executed in open court,—the demandant or grantee claiming a piece of land, the defendant or grantor by agreement assenting or being silent, and the magistrate giving judgment for the demandant. The memorial which was made of the transfer was termed *transactio*,* and had the authority of *res judicata*, for every person who could claim any interest in the land was one of the *pares curiæ*, and in apprehension of law was present at the time the feoffment was made. His silence was consent. Hence the consequences of this mode of conveyance, which destroys all contingent estates, limitations, and conditions.

When the feoffment was executed in a court of record it was termed a *Fine*. That the feoffment was used to transfer incorporeal rights as well as lands is shown by this circumstance: that, in a suit for an advowson, the demandant used the words of Gaius above cited. Mr. Reeves has given a precedent of such a declaration.†

Partition by decree of a court, or *adjudicatio*, was another species of conveyance, peculiar to citizens. The action, "quæ discitur familiæ heriscundæ locum

* Glan. fol. 61.

† Vol. I. p. 137.

habet inter eos qui communem hæreditatem, &c., et inter cohæredes ubi agitur de proparte sororum vel inter alios ubi res inter partes et cohæredes dividi debeat," &c.* The Roman Law had also an action *de communi dividundo*, which differed so little from the former, *familiæ heriscundæ*, that it was thought by the compilers of the Digest unnecessary to treat of them separately. "Adeo affines sunt, ut de his simul agere necessarium." † Coke in the above extract does not notice this distinction, and treats these two actions as one. The Digest explains that the *actio familiæ* is "actio quæ cohæredi adversus cohæredes datur ut dividatur hæreditatem. Actio autem communi dividundo est actio quæ inter eos qui quascunque res *præter* hæreditatem communes ac indivisos habeat datur ut illæ res inter eos dividantur." At Common Law, as in the Civil, the *actio familiæ* is exclusively applicable to coparceners or coheirs. They derive their name from the fact that they may, whilst tenants in common and joint tenants cannot at Common Law, be compelled to make partition. ‡ The word *heriscundæ* is a corruption of the word *ercendo*, — the ancient form of *coercendo*, from *coerceo*, to compel. Gaius states that this action was derived from the law of the Twelve Tables, "de hæreditatibus et de tutelis." §

The Common and Civil Law continue in all the consequences of this mode of partition to be identical. Thus, there must be equality of partition, — each warrants the share of the other. Where the property is indivisible it is given to one, subject to the pay-

* 1 Co. Litt. 783.

† Vol. IV. p. 534, Poth. ed.

‡ 1 Co. Litt. 783, 869, 911.

§ Dig. I. 421.

ment to the other of the value of his share.* In like manner, both systems recognize partition by lot and arbitrament. Littleton mentions that other incident of partition known as Hotchpot. The Common Law confined it to land given in frank marriage. In the Civil Law it comprehended every advancement of the father to his child, and was known as the *collatio bonorum.* Domat discusses the whole subject with his usual ability and learning.†

CHAPTER XXVII.

POSSESSION.

"To suppose a state of man," says Chancellor Kent, "prior to the existence of any notions of separate property, when all things were common, and when men throughout the world lived without law or government, in innocence and simplicity, is quite fanciful, if it be not altogether a dream of the imagination."‡ The learned author then goes on to state, that occupancy is the *natural* and original method of acquiring property in lands and movables. Certainly the Common Law rejects all such notions, and holds property to be of positive institution and not derived from any other source. Our system does not permit us to enter into the refinements which the modern civilians discuss, as to

---

* 1 Co. Litt. 814, 826; Dig. 5. 24. 30.

† Vol. II. p. 662.

‡ 2 Com., Lect. 34.

the question whether occupation does or does not confer a right. All lands belong either to the state or an individual, and the occupant without title is a trespasser. The lapse of time will not bar the remedy of the former, but it will of the individual, and in the latter case only by virtue of positive legislation. Until the remedy is completely barred, the occupant is as much a trespasser as he was at the moment he entered upon the land. Moreover, the public law interferes not for the sake of the individual, but to preserve the public peace; the advantage to the occupant is incidental. There are questions growing out of the loss of remedy to the rightful owner, which, it is believed, have not yet been settled by judicial opinion. Thus, where a person by adverse possession can defend himself against the true owner, if he dies without heirs, shall the land escheat to the state, or does it revert to the former rightful owner? Is the right to the land extinguished, or only the remedy for its recovery taken away, by the statutes of limitation? In the analogous case of a debt, although the remedy may be barred, yet the right to the money, the consideration, still exists so far that a new promise will revive the right of action. There are numerous other cases in which the same rule is admitted. A principal difficulty in the way of considering the right as unextinguished is that interpretation of the statutes of limitation concerning lands, which makes them, not only means of defence, but of acquisition. But that view is founded upon the assumption that there is a law of nature which justifies man in occupying lands within the territory of an established state. It is a law, however, that is not tolerated where the public is concerned.

The Civil Law recognized three kinds of occupation, — that with just title, that with a supposed just title, and, lastly, mere tortious occupation. By that system these three classes had appropriate and specific remedies. And the division is manifestly not without some show of reason. But the Common Law notices only the first and last of them. The word *possession* is used by our legal writers to express, not only the occupation of a rightful owner, but also that of a wrong-doer, — the *pedis possessor.* But it is apprehended that it is properly applicable only to the former, and certainly has that grammatical sense. The possessor, by whom is meant the rightful owner, has, — 1. A right of property; 2. Occupation by himself, or his agents or tenants. To acquire the first, contract is necessary; to acquire the second, investiture or livery. Livery is continually confounded with seizin by writers, but they differ as much as cause and effect; it is by livery that seizin is obtained.* The possession of a feud is seizin, — possession is synonymous with seizin. It is in this sense that Britton states that a frank tenement is the possession of a feud.†

The right of property, together with actual occupation, was not sufficient to make a frank tenement; investiture also was indispensable. Investiture was an act of sovereignty, whether it concerned the creation of a principality, a title of honor, or a tenancy in fee simple. It was the solemn and public delivery of the land, an approval of the contract by the sovereign, whether king or lord, in the presence of the peers of the person to whom it was granted. Hence,

---

* 1 Cruise, 63.

† C. 32.

if a person having acquired the right of property entered upon the land without investiture, he was a trespasser. His entry might be *clandestina*, *clam*, secretly, and the remedy was, as Bracton states,* a writ of intrusion, which might be purchased when one *ratione alicujus chartæ* entered without livery. The Civil Law was in this respect identical with the Common Law. Bracton uses the very words of that system. Domat states, that if a person who had acquired a title entered upon the land clandestinely, that is, without the knowledge of the person by whom opposition might be made, he was a wrong-doer.†

It is not unimportant now to have a correct knowledge of these principles. For although the solemn form of investiture is no longer observed, yet the substance of it still remains. Inattention to them will certainly lead into error. We will show this, and at the same time elucidate some of the leading rules of the law of descents. Mr. Reeves, in his History of the Common Law, ‡ a work of considerable authority, states that seizin was merely possession, meaning thereby occupation. So that a tortious occupier had possession or seizin. Nothing can be more incorrect than this statement; feudal history and judicial authority contradict it. || Again he states, "that another (possession) was a precarious and clandestine possession attended with violence." Passing by the contradiction of a clandestine possession attended by violence, he plainly confuses three different kinds of occupation, the precarious, the clandestine, and the violent, —*precaria, clam, vi et armis*. The last two,

---

* Lib. 4, fol. 160. † Lib. 3, tit. 7, s. 12. ‡ Vol. I. p. 177.
|| Bracton, fol. 38, 160; 1 Burr. 107; 1 Cruise, 12.

moreover, are acquired against the consent, and the first with the permission, of the true owner. "Item est quædam possessio precaria ut si quis concesserit alicui habitationem," &c.* To this class originally belonged, as we have seen, tenants for years, at will, and by sufferance. It followed necessarily from this error, that Mr. Reeves should not understand, not only the rules, but the history, of the Common Law.

Another illustration of the consequence of neglecting the fundamental principles of the Common Law will be found in the criticism of Mr. Stephens in the explanation given by Mr. Blackstone of the maxim, "Non jus sed seisina facit stipitem." The former remarks that the solution of the latter is unsatisfactory. The passage of Blackstone is in these words: "We must also remember that no person can properly be such an ancestor as that an inheritance of lands and tenements can be derived from him unless he hath *actual* seizin of such lands, either by his own entry," &c. Mr. Stephens says that the origin of this rule has never been satisfactorily traced, and that, though Blackstone's explanation may sufficiently show why the descent was not derived except from a person who had obtained *actual* seizin, yet it does not show why the person seized was to be *propositus* or root of the descent in preference to a purchaser who has obtained actual seizin. For instance, suppose this case: A dies seized, leaving B his heir; now if B dies without having obtained seizin, the heir of A, and not of B, will inherit the estate. Here B, being next in blood, might obtain seizin, but, failing to do so, he does not become the

---

* Bracton, Lib. 2, fol. 39.

propositus. If to this case we add another element, and suppose that B, in his lifetime, conveyed his right to a *bonâ fide* purchaser, who enters into actual occupation, and then B dies, never having had seizin, Mr. Stephens informs us that the heir of A has the right to enter and eject the purchaser, and that the reason of this is unexplainable by himself or Mr. Blackstone.

The difficulty in the solution of the question consists solely in this, that, like Mr. Reeves, they confound seizin with actual occupation. Actual seizin is their phrase. But seizin consists of three things, the right of property, actual occupation, and the consent of the lord.* When a person has seizin in this sense, he is the *propositus*. The purchaser in the case put had the right, the actual occupation, but not investiture; and without the latter, occupation with right did not constitute a good title. In the language of the maxim, "Non jus sed seisina facet stipitem." For example, suppose the case of a tenant who conveys his feud to another; although this contract was obligatory between them, the purchaser could not enter without the consent of the lord under whom the tenant held. Again, in the same way, and no other, is to be explained the maxim, "Possessio fratris de feodo simplici, facet sororem hæredem." It is only necessary to observe that the phrase *possessio de feodo simplici* is a paraphrase of the word *seisina*. Now upon these two maxims nearly the whole Common Law of descents depends. Mr. Brown, in his work on the leading maxims of the law, mentions only one other on this branch,

---

* 1 Cruise, 41.

"Hæreditas non ascendit." This implies the existence of the first that we have noticed, and is only indicative of the person who may demand seizin. Misapprehension, therefore, of the true reasons of these maxims cannot but prevent satisfactory explanations of questions of law. "The reason of the law is the life of the law; for though a man can tell the law, yet, if he know not the reasons thereof, he soon shall forget his superficial knowledge. But when he findeth the right reason of the law . . . . . this will not only serve him for the understanding of the particular case, but of many others."

Investiture did not confer jurisdiction. The law attributed jurisdiction to property, and that without the intervention either of the donor or the donee. The omission to distinguish between this attribute and the investiture has conduced to, if it has not altogether produced, the confusion which we have heretofore noticed as existing in the use of the word *fee*. After the lord had created a limited estate, he still retained jurisdiction; and if we suppose that the tenant of the limited estate made a subinfeudation, he also had jurisdiction over his sub-tenant. Thus, in regular succession from the sovereign to the lowest baron, jurisdiction belonged to the donor. Every feud was a miniature copy of the state.

CHAPTER XXVIII.

RETROSPECT.

The inquiry which we have made has exhibited the fact that the Common Law in all its parts, political, civil, and social, rests upon the principle of the attribution of sovereignty or political power to the proprietors of lands. They alone possessed a voice in the government, — the right of representation, of imposing taxes, of holding high places. The non-landholder was impotent. Time has greatly modified this law, even in England; but property is still there the source of power. In this country much has already been done to take away all direct influence from property; its indirect influence, in the shape of corruption, must continue, and history teaches us that it will increase, as population becomes more dense. The utility of this change, from the direct to the indirect, the wisdom of reversing the Common Law rule of attributing power to landed property, are questions without the scope of the present inquiry. But it may be observed that, at the bottom, they really resolve themselves into the question of the best form of government. A great statesman, lately deceased, has stated with great clearness and force the arguments in favor of the concurrent majority, — the union of numbers and taxation, — power and property. His disquisitions are not, in this respect, novel in theory, but old, and approved by the experience of a great and happy and highly civilized people. But it may, nevertheless, be utterly inconsistent with the very different form of government under which we live. Right or wrong, it does present for our consideration the gravest question which can employ the thoughts of any people.

It is also to be observed, that in proportion as this principle has ceased to be practically operative in the law, will the legal system of these States differ from the ancient Common Law. We may continue to term it the Common Law after the attribution of jurisdiction to property is no longer remembered except by antiquarians, but it will not be the Common Law. A new system, having a different basis, tendency, nature, and results, will grow up; and if it is cultivated with the aid of English books which recognize as a fundamental principle what is rejected by us, our system must be bent from its natural tendency, and so be deformed. That American law may perhaps be better calculated than its original to protect man in the development of his moral and mental qualities. Under its shadow he may enjoy, in larger proportion than his ancestors, those blessings which good laws and good government defend, but do not create. But these are not certain results. Even the advocates of human perfectibility do not contend that an entire departure from the experience of the past is either desirable in itself or proper to attain their promised condition of perfection. They teach the possibility of human development reaching perfection, not the necessity of complete revolution, either in public or private law.

Moreover, the private law must, in a greater or less degree, be assimilated to the public. "At jus privatum sub tutela juris publici," says Lord Bacon.

Then it is not less a momentous question to individuals, What will be the consequence to private property of the recognition of the principle that political power does not belong to property? Some bold theorists have already announced the consequences; and, admitting it to be true that numbers, the majority, are the rightful owners of the power of the state, it will be difficult to refute the inference that they may dispose of the whole state, and therefore of every part of it. Power is human will, — applied to things it creates property, and has the masterdom and disposition of it. Why, then, should the rightful owners of the power, the life, of the state, not participate in the property which sustains that life? Why should the state not feed upon the property of the state? All men are equal, — one generation cannot bind another, — governments may be changed at pleasure, — the majority can do no wrong. These are principles which seem not uninteresting to the possessors of property. It is possible that the fundamental maxim of the Common Law is unjust to mankind. Certainly the architects of it did not intrust the preservation of property to those who might have an interest in its destruction.

CHAPTER XXIX.

THE TENDENCY OF THE AMERICAN LAW.

The British Colonies in North America were connected together by a common allegiance to one crown, and in reference to it they were one people. Their internal condition also tended towards unity. From their first settlement they possessed the manners, knowledge, and refined modes of thought which belong to a highly improved state of civilization. They knew no barbarous age in which the germs of their institutions originated. They had brought with them from the mother country the general principles of free government and the leading maxims of her jurisprudence. They all adopted them, with such modifications as a change of country required. No dissimilarities existed or grew up among them, such as distinguish the Scotch or Irish or Welsh from the English. The inhabitants were almost altogether alike, with some shades of difference in matters of religion; but sectarian dispute had never been inflamed into civil strife. Hence, when they threw off their political allegiance, the Puritan and his antagonist, the Episcopalian, — the Roman Catholic and the Huguenot fugitive from Roman Catholic power, — freely and voluntarily pledged to each other their lives and sacred honor to accomplish a revolution that should establish a free government, which, whilst it tolerated every form, denied, what each had aimed to attain, superiority to any form, of sectarianism. This fact alone proves incontestably, that in heart, customs, laws, institutions, and political principles, the inhabitants of the provinces were one people.

The Articles of Confederation, therefore, had no such difficult task to perform as had the laws of the Middle Ages, or of Edward the Confessor, — to blend diverse races, who had never before stood face to face but as foes, into one harmonious people. The revolt of the Colonies disturbed, but did not destroy, the internal governments and established laws of the States. The Articles supplied partially the want of a common political tie. And when experience led to their abandonment, it was not because the internal, but the external, relations of the States required it. Undoubtedly, as they operated only upon the States in their collective capacity, and could not directly affect the people, they created a government weak at home and abroad. In legal formula, it may be said that the fiction of the unity of the federal government had for its basis the fiction of the unities of each State. This was the defect in the Confederation of 1781. The ninth article, which contains all the provisions for the settlement of questions between the States and between individuals, makes no alterations in the private laws of the States. These were unchanged.

The Constitution of 1787, which was intended to correct the defects of the Articles of Confederation, and to form a more perfect union, invests the general government with jurisdiction over the States, and in certain cases over the people of the States. But it does not, nor was it its design to, alter the existing private laws of the state further than was necessary to preserve consistency between the public and the private law. The Constitution is in fact the great statute of each State; an essential part of its private law, and nearly the whole of its public law. It is the supreme law, but not the fundamental law, in the sense of *fons publici privatique juris.* Its enactment produced less change in the laws of a State, than Magna Charta did in the Common Law. Apart from political considerations, the questions reserved for the exclusive cognizance of the courts of the United States were all within the competency, and might have been left to the decision, of the State courts. But the distinction between exclusive and concurrent jurisdiction was made, and the cases falling under either head may be ascertained, as has been already suggested, by reference to the ends and means of accomplishing them.

The direct influence of the Constitution, as a public statute, upon the laws of the several States, has been much less than its indirect. The Common Law was recognized as the law of the land, but modified to suit the circumstances of the people of the Colonies. The courts, however, untrammelled by local and customary rules, which were venerable only for their antiquity, or which by prescription had become property, were at liberty, and often were compelled, to reinvestigate questions already decided in England, and for the purposes of inquiry to resort to foreign laws, universal reason, and colonial utility. Many, perhaps most, of the more eminent lawyers of the Colonies, down to the Revolution, were educated in England, and no doubt studied the Common Law, with the improvements which Lord Mansfield was then introducing. "It may be observed," says Chancellor Kent," and with greater width of truth of this country than of England, that a very large proportion of the matter contained in the old reporters prior to the English Revolution has been superseded, and is now cast into the shade by the improvements of modern times; by the cultivation of maritime jurisdiction; by the growing value and variety of personal property; by the spirit of commerce, and the enlargement of equity jurisdiction; by the introduction of more liberal and enlightened views of public policy, and, in short, by the study and influence of the Civil Law." * The same causes, which were thus both in England and in the Colonies producing great alterations in the Common Law, received new energy and impetus from the Constitution. The law of the Colonies already conformed to a much greater extent than that of England to the *jus gentium*. Now, as has been seen, the principle of the Common Law which attributes jurisdiction to property, and denies it to those who are not landlords, renders the state a close corporation. In England the principle had been so modified as to attribute a share of jurisdiction to every native, but the alien, although encouraged to visit the kingdom for the purposes of commerce, found so many difficulties in the way of obtaining the privilege of citizenship, that he rarely asked for it. Their total exclusion practically preserved something of the spirit of municipalism in the law, — the state was still a corporation. The right of membership could be obtained only with difficulty, and generally only on public considerations.

But the Colonists had so little of the pride of citizenship in them, that they regarded England as their home, and America as a sort of decent asylum for the

* I. 453, 454.

poor. Emigration was universally encouraged, and lands granted without any previous probation. The Constitution accorded with the sentiments of the people; it did not declare what should constitute citizenship, — it did not limit Congress in its power to enact naturalization laws. Hence we have naturalized citizens who have become such as individuals, after a probation of five years supposed to be passed in learning to love and admire our institutions, and we have naturalized citizens who have become such as nations, having for our laws and institutions only such love as is felt by the conquered for the conqueror. When Congress, therefore, limited the probationary period to ten, seven, or five years, a mere point of time in the life of a nation, and also made citizenship depend entirely upon the pleasure of the alien to take it, citizenship ceased to be a privilege. This, with many other proximate causes, but all ultimately referable to the severance of jurisdiction from property, has carried the public and private law onward *towards* the entire abandonment of municipalism. The political consequences of the extension of citizenship to all who will become inhabitants of these States, are not within our consideration. But history is not silent, and furnishes thoughts which deserve to be meditated upon.

In addition to these external and political causes of change in the Common Law, there are others of an internal nature. Its history presents to that of the Civil Law this contrast, that the Common Law is confined to the Anglo-Norman race. Whilst they spread their dominion over the face of the earth, they do not spread their municipal law. It is not the ardent desire of any of their conquered subjects to be governed by it. Their own people, as colonists, reject it. The inherent defect is its want of the power of self-defence. Its municipalism is merely conservatism, and has no element of progress, — and without their union nothing moral can be permanent. Self-defence includes the power to be offensive, — to destroy for the purpose of self-preservation. But this is not the case with the Common Law of England. It is modified by contact with other laws, but never has impressed upon any of them its peculiarities. Now this does not arise from any narrowness of the principles of the law of property, for these are no more English than Roman or French. But from the perpetuation of the principle, that to property alone belongs jurisdiction, — its political law. So, in the like manner, all that was peculiar to Rome expired with the fall of the Republic, and that which was common to humanity, the law of nature, was perpetuated.

Another cause is, that the Common Law is eminently technical. In no other known system have formulas so powerful an effect. Fictions of the law are all equitable, and approve themselves to our natural reason; formulas are unmeaning except to those who have attained to "an artificial perfection of reason, gotten by long study, observation, and experience." Thus, that an estate granted to a person with the word *heirs* annexed should create in him an absolute inheritance, has no foundation in natural reason. Nor does this formula admit of accurate translation into the common language of literature, — Latin. The proof of this is given by Bracton: after stating a limitation to A, and *hæredibus sui corporis*, he informs us that they take by descent "quamvis quibusdam videatur quod ipsi feoffati fuerint cum parentibus; quod non est verum." * The reason of this opinion that he condemns is plain. Those who thought that the heirs of the body took joint interests with their parent gave the same meaning to these words, *hæredibus sui corporis*, that civilians give to *sui hæredes.* The latter mean children, — lineal descendants, and so heirs of the body *naturaliter*, — and used in that sense the children would take joint interests with their parents, as was decided in Wild's case. The error was in not perceiving that the limitation was a formula having a very different meaning from that which the words convey according to their idiomatic use. So the difference between the formula of a person dying leaving no issue, and leaving no issue living at the time of his death, is untranslatable, and even to the well-educated scholar of Continental Europe unintelligible. It is manifest that formulas do not commend themselves to the natural reason of mankind, and therefore cannot become the property of humanity. They are the mere husks of the law. But as the peculiarities of the Common Law of real estate are formulas, they too are destined to continue exceptional, if they do not disappear even from that system.

---

* Lib. 2, fol. 18.

CHAPTER XXX.

CONCLUSION.

THE analysis of the fundamental principles of the Common Law has been made. It has been shown that our system is not "a shapeless mass of materials," as has been supposed by very eminent European jurists; and that there is a principle pervading it uniting together all parts of society, and controlling the state and the family, the beginning and the end of humanity; — that the same bond which unites many in society unites two in marriage; — that in whatever light we view these, the chief relations of human existence, comprehending *omnes omnium charitates*, it may be said with the utmost truth and accuracy, both of society and of marriage, that each is *omnis vitæ consortium, divini humanique juris communicatio.*

Our exposition has traced the rules of the law of real estate to the mixed law of the Middle Ages. Occasion has also been taken to exhibit some of the more important analogies between the Common and Civil Law, and to indicate the particular instances in which courts of justice and law writers were obliged to adopt such rules of the latter as were not inconsistent with the political principles of the former. The affinities of the two systems would perhaps justify a more extended examination, but it is sufficient to say that it is a matter of well-founded surprise that the Common Law judges have so frequently resorted to the Civil, and that it has been tolerated to so great a degree. For the hostility to the introduction of the Civil as the *corpus juris* of England was most natural and proper, and the attempt by the clergy exhibited, not only their ambition, but their ignorance of the Civil Law and the then existing condition of political affairs. As the Normans had no law suited to their condition at the time of their invasion of France, they readily adopted the mixed law. But it was far different three hundred years afterwards, when a portion of them, having established laws and a well-ordered government, took possession of England. Then they had a code suited to their new relations, and therefore with ancestral pride adhered to it. The change that was desirable, and that which they attempted, was to reconcile their conquered subjects to the feudal law which they themselves could not abandon without ruin. Only the slow progress of time could extinguish the hatred of the Saxon to the Norman. But the latter had no national antagonism to the Civil Law; on the contrary, their Continental brethren received it, as their predecessors had done, as a subsidiary law to explain and interpret the mixed law. And so thoroughly were the Normans changed in their manners, laws, and language by their conquest of Normandy, that they "were regarded both by Saxons and Danes as not only a different nation, but actually a different race. The historians of Denmark speak of the Norman conquerors of England as a people of *Roman* or *Latin* race, and deplore the conquest as a triumph of the Roman blood over the Teutonic." * All the tribes that acquired permanent settlements were alike

* Thucydides, by Arnold, Vol. II. p. 55, note.

transformed, and adopted the Civil Law, — in the northern part of France as subsidiary, and in the southern part as the *lex scripta*. The conduct of the clergy, therefore, could lead only to failure. Their ignorance of the true spirit of the Civil Law was equally manifest. No nation that has ever existed, no code that has ever been contrived, are so tolerant of national customs. The Pandects will furnish a multitude of passages in which it is enjoined upon provincial rulers to respect local customs, and to maintain them with their authority, unless political interests demanded their abrogation. It was upon this very ground that the Northern barbarians so readily adopted it. The alternative view was not presented to them, to abandon their own customs and accept the Roman laws. It was in a similar spirit that the Conqueror agreed to tolerate the Saxon laws, whilst he enforced his own code. When, therefore, the barons rejected the proposition of the clergy to abandon their native customs, they responded not only in the language, but in the spirit, of the Pandects. At the same time, our juridical history shows that courts and writers daily and openly appealed to that code to aid them in the interpretation of their laws.

Finally, I have endeavored to show that our system of jurisprudence consists of many subordinate parts, all of which are connected by beautiful dependencies, and each of them, as I have fully persuaded myself, is reducible to a few plain elements, that will commend themselves to our natural reason, or be justified by the history and situation of our political ancestors. But if the law be merely an unconnected series of decisions and statutes, its use may remain, though its dignity as a science be lost. Reason must yield its supremacy to memory, and the *cantor formularum* is the greatest of lawyers.

THE END.

Reprints of the Legal Classics Published by The Lawbook Exchange, Ltd.

☙*Legal Treatises* ☙

Elements of Medical Jurisprudence. *Theodric Romeyn Beck.* Albany: Websters and Skinners, 1823. Two volumes. xxxiv, 418; viii, [9]-471 pp. Reprinted 1997 by The Lawbook Exchange, Ltd. ISBN 1-886363-24-2. Cloth. $125.

* Beck's treatise was the first significant American work on forensic medicine. Embracing "all that is really useful either to the physician or the lawyer," Beck's work supplanted both Smith's *Principles of Forensic Medicine* (1821) and Paris and Fonblanque's *Medical Jurisprudence* (1823) as the preeminent text in the English language. Beck graduated from the New York College of Physicians and Surgeons in 1811, and his work became an authority when the field was in its earliest stages. In volume one, Beck treats feigned and disqualifying diseases, impotence and sterility, doubtful sex, rape, pregnancy, delivery, infanticide (contributed by his brother, Dr. John Beck), legitimacy, survivorship, age and identity, and mental alienation; volume two examines persons found dead, wounds, and poisons, whether mineral, vegetable or animal. At the beginning of the work is a useful bibliography of texts consulted by Beck. Indexed.

A Treatise of the Law of Judgments. [Fifth edition]. *A.C. Freeman. Edited by Edward W. Tuttle.* San Francisco: Bancroft-Whitney, 1925. Three volumes. 1216; 1280; 1264 pp. Reprinted 1993 by The Lawbook Exchange, Ltd. ISBN 0-9630106-6-2. Cloth. $295.

* Considered by Vanderbilt to be one of the great textbooks in which "the history of American law might

well be traced." *Men and Measures in the Law*, p. 21. "In the present treatise (which cites over 35,000 cases), the editor has analyzed the cases with care.... The book will be of great assistance to lawyers searching for authorities in the important field it covers. *Harvard Law Review* 32(2):283-5.

A Treatise on Equity Jurisprudence. [Fifth Edition]. *John N. Pomeroy. Edited by Spencer W. Symons.* San Francisco and New York: Bancroft-Whitney and Lawyers Cooperative, 1941. Five volumes. 914; 1134; 1063; 1104; 716 pp. Reprinted 1995 by The Lawbook Exchange, Ltd. ISBN 1-886363-05-6. Cloth. $450.

* Still being cited in the highest appellate courts, "[o]ne of the main strengths of Pomeroy is the treatment of the fundamental principles or maxims of equity: that treatment is unrivalled in any modern equity text." Peter McDermott, *International Trade and Business Law Annual 2(2):297 (1996).* "Few modern textbooks are of permanent value. Pomeroy's *Equity Jurisprudence* is an exception." Albert J. Beveridge in Vanderbilt, *Studying Law*, p. 27. "As a book of reference, indeed, it will outrank the *Restatements*.... As an encyclopedia, too, Pomeroy is useful as indicating some of the reaches of our equitable process." *Virginia Law Review*, 29:507-9.

Legal History

The Black Book of the Admiralty, with an Appendix. Monumenta Juridica. *Edited by Sir Travers Twiss.* London: Longman & Co. and Trubner & Co., 1871. Four volumes. 4, xciii, 491, [2]; 4, lxxxvii, 500, 31; 4, lxxxvi, 673, [1], 31; 4, clii, 559, 32 pp. Reprinted June 1998 by The Lawbook Exchange, Ltd. LC 97-38809 ISBN 1-886363-39-0. Cloth. $495.

The earliest records of the court of Admiralty portray not only the origin of maritime law as we know it today, but are also important records of the origin of international law due to the court of Admiralty's jurisdiction over commercial contracts and foreign trade. This set contains documents from many sources collected by an official of the Admiralty during the reign of Henry VI. Includes regulations regarding the criminal jurisdiction of the Admiralty, the rights of the crown, the Admiralty droits; rights, wages, prizes, merchant contracts, collissions, inquests; a tract on the ordo judiciorum illustrating the court's model from civil rather than common law procedure; and the inquisition taken at Queensborough in 1375. This edition contains the laws of Oleron with eleven additional rules; and an Appendix of documents including the statutes of Richard II and Henry IV's reign concerning Admiralty jurisdiction.

Citizenship Sovereignty. *John S. Wright.* Chicago: Published for American Citizens, the True Maintainers of State Sovereignty, 1864. xxiv, 208pp. Reprinted September 1998 by The Lawbook Exchange, Ltd. LC 98-15940 ISBN 1-886363-55-2. Cloth. $65.
* Defines and examines the concept of citizenship and its relation to the sovereignty of this nation and of states.

Compiled Laws of the Cherokee Nation. Tahlequah, I.T.:National Advocate Print, 1881. 370pp. Reprinted September 1998 by The Lawbook Exchange, Ltd. With a new introduction by Michael Weber. LC 98-12741. ISBN 1-886363-42-0Cloth. $60.
* This volume provides a unique legal and historical record. It is an exact reprint of an 1881 compilation, originally published by the Cherokee National Council, of "the laws of the Cherokee Nation now in force." These laws -- the 1839 constitution of the Cherokee Nation and the basic laws passed under it – provided the framework for the government of the Cherokee Nation from 1839 until the early 1900s, when the Cherokees' independence

was ended by the United States Congress. These documents are sure to be of enormous interest to legal historians.

The story of the Cherokees is both one of immense tragedy and unique achievement. Within scarcely more than a generation, the Cherokees consciously transformed themselves from being a society that lived under an age-old, unwritten set of norms and traditional cultural practices to one governed by a written constitution and code of statutes. The Cherokees made this transformation in the vain hope that it would make it easier for them to live peacefully surrounded by the United States. They closely modeled their constitution in most respects on the United States Constitution. Yet there are some fascinating differences concerning the judiciary and land ownership.

Contained in this volume are the Cherokees' 1839 constitution along with amendments to it necessitated by the 1866 treaty between the Cherokee Nation and the United States; the 1838 Act of Union between the Cherokee Nation and the United States; the 1838 Act of Union between the Eastern and Western Cherokees; numerous basic laws and miscellaneous acts covering a huge variety of subjects from the duties of the principal chief to the killing of game; agreements between the Cherokees and the Creeks and Osages, Delawares, and Shawnees; and an appendix containing documents relating to the boundaries of the Cherokee Nation as defined by agreements with the United States.

The Criminal Prosecution and Capital Punishment of Animals. *E.P. Evans.* New York: E.P. Dutton, 1906. x, 384pp. Reprinted August 1998 by The Lawbook Exchange, Ltd. LC 98-12801. ISBN 1-886363-52-8. Cloth. $65.

* This pioneering work in English, brings together an amazing assemblage of court cases in which animals have been amed as defendants -- chickens, rats, field mice,

bees, gnats, and (in 34 recorded instances) pigs, among others--providing insight into such modern issues as animal rights, capital punishment, and social and criminal theory. Evans' suggests an intriguing distinction between trials of specific animals or particular crimes (the "murder" of an infant by a pig, for example) and trials of animals for larger, catastrophic events such as plagues and infestations. In the latter case, Evans suggests a parallel to witchcraft.

The Doctor and Student or Dialogues Between a Doctor of Divinity and a Student in the Laws of England Containing the Grounds of Those Laws Together with Questions and Cases Concerning the Equity Thereof Revised and Corrected by William Muchall, Gent. to which are added two pieces concerning Suits in Chancery by Subpoena. *[Christopher Saint Germain]* [1460-1540]. Cincinnati:Robert Clarke & Co., 1874. xiv, 401pp. Reprinted August 1998 by The Lawbook Exchange, Ltd. LC 98-11338. ISBN 1-886363-49-8. Cloth. $65.
* Written originally in Latin in 1523, this work contains two dialogues between a doctor of divinity and a student of English law, and is known for putting into popular form canonist learning regarding the nature and object of law, the religious and moral standards of law, the foundations of the common law and other discussions regarding the jurisidiction of Parliament. A very important work in the development of equity, *Doctor and Student* appeared in numerous editions. It was frequently cited and influenced generations of legal writers down to Blackstone and later. Marke 38. HLC II:516-517.

Essays in Law and History. *William S. Holdsworth. Edited by A.L. Goodhart and H.G. Hanbury.* Oxford: At the Clarendon Press, 1946. xv, 302 pp. Reprinted 1995 by The Lawbook Exchange, Ltd. ISBN 1-886363-13-7.

* This volume collects seventeen essays the great legal scholar wrote over the course of his very prolific career. Topics chosen include martial law, the English constitution, case law, equity, trusts, libel, law reporting in the nineteenth- and twentieth-centuries, contract and land law, among others. "The constitutional historian, the international lawyer, the real property expert, the common law practitioner, the civilian and even the general reader will each find something to his address. It is a book to browse and enjoy at leisure." *Law Quarterly Review* 64:120-2. The book concludes with a table of cases and name and general indexes.

A General Survey of Events, Sources, Persons & Movements in Continental Legal History. By Various European Authors. A General Survey of Events, Sources, Persons & Movements in Continental Legal History. By Various European Authors. With an introduction by Albert Kocourek. Boston: Little, Brown, 1912. liii, 754pp. Reprinted September 1998 by The Lawbook Exchange, Ltd. LC 98-11159. ISBN 1-886363-47-1. Cloth. $110.
* Originally published as part of The Continental Legal History Series under the auspices of the Association of American Law Schools. A survey of legal history in Western Europe from medieval to modern times, the work includes translations into English from leading authorities on European legal history such as Carlo Calisse, Jean Brissaud, Heinrich Brunner, Richard Schroeder, Rafael Altimara and Frederick W. Maitland. Marke 133.

Great Jurists of the World. *Edited by Sir John MacDonell and Edward Manson. With an Introduction by Van Vechten Veeder.* Boston: Little, Brown, and Company, 1914. Illustrated. xxxii, 607 pp. Reprinted 1997 by The Lawbook Exchange, Ltd. ISBN 1-886363-28-5. Cloth. $95.

* Originally published under the auspices of the Association of American Law Schools in the Continental Legal History Series. (1914). Ranging over a period of two thousand years, the work covers the lives and chief works of selected eminent jurists such as Gaius, Papinian, Domitius Ulpian, Bartolus, Andrea Alciati and his Predecessors, Jacques Cujas, Albericus Gentilis, Francis Bacon, Hugo Grotius, John Selden, Thomas Hobbes, Richard Zouche, Jean Baptiste Colbert, Gottfried Wilhelm von Liebnitz, Samuel von Puffendorf, Giovanni Battista Vico, Cornelius van Bynkershoek, Charles Louis de Secondat, Robert Joseph Pothier, Emerich de Vattel, Caesar Bonesana, William Scott, Jeremy Bentham, Carl Joseph Anton Mittermaier, Freidrich Carl von Savigny, and Rudolph von Jhering.

The History of American Customs Jurisprudence. *William H. Futrell.* New York: Published privately, 1941. 314pp. Reprinted August 1998 by The Lawbook Exchange, Ltd. LC 98-11342. ISBN 1-886363-51-X. Cloth. $60.
* Originally privately printed and scarce, this work gives the historic background of the powers derived from the Constitution and covers all aspects of U.S. customs law. Pound commended it as "a thoroughly workmanlike job."

Historians of Anglo-American Law. *W.S. Holdsworth.* New York: Columbia University Press, 1928. 175 pp. Reprinted 1994 by The Lawbook Exchange, Ltd. ISBN 0-9630106-9-7. Cloth. $40.
* In chronological order, beginning with Coke and Selden, Holdsworth surveys the work of the great practitioners of Anglo-American legal history. No one interested in the growth of Anglo-American law can fail to read with pleasure and profit this stimulating treatment of the development of legal history.

The History of English Law. Before the Time of Edward I. [Second edition]. *Frederick Pollock and Frederic William Maitland.* Cambridge: Cambridge University Press, 1898. Two volumes. xxxviii, 688; xiv, 691 pp. Reprinted 1996 by The Lawbook Exchange, Ltd. ISBN 1-886363-22-6. Cloth. $165.

* Professors Maitland of Cambridge and Pollock of Oxford joined forces (although Maitland is credited with the lion's share) to write what has been termed an epoch-making work. The authors elucidate the origins of English law, providing for the first time a systematic presentation of the early stages of its evolution. The first volume gives an historical overview, beginning with ecclesiastical law and proceeding to cover Anglo-Saxon law, Norman law, Roman and Canon law, and law in the time of Glanvill and Bracton. The second treats the doctrines of English law, including all aspects of tenure, the law of personal condition, status, and estate, and the jurisdiction and the communities of the land. Clear exposition and countless references make this an essential book for anyone interested in early English law.

The History of Lawyers. Ancient and Modern. *William Forsyth.* Boston: Estes & Lauriat, 1875. Illustrated. xvii, 404 pp. Reprinted 1996 by the Lawbook Exchange, Ltd. ISBN 1-886363-14-5. Cloth. $60.

* First published in 1849 in London under the title, *Hortensius:* or, *The Advocate*, Forsyth's *History of Lawyers* is a spirited account of advocacy in ancient Greece, Rome, and England and of the bar in France. Acknowledging that "[w]e are too apt to cloth the ancients in buckram, and view them, as it were, through a magnifying glass, so that they loom before us in the dim distance in almost colossal proportions," Forsyth presents in familiar terms the language of the law and how advocates behaved. Frequently citing classical sources with his own

translations, he describes in impressive detail such things as curious trials and the rights and obligations of counsel. Chapter headings include: *The Athenian Courts*; *Advocacy in Ancient Rome*; *The Bar under the Empire and in the Middle Ages*; *The Noblesse de la Robe*; *The Honorarium*; ad, *Forensic Casuistry*.

History of Trial by Jury. [Second edition]. *William Forsyth.* Jersey City: Frederick D. Linn, [1875]. x, 388 pp. Reprinted 1994 by The Lawbook Exchange, Ltd. ISBN 0-9630106-8-9. Cloth. $50.
* First published in England in 1852, Forsyth's *Trial by Jury* is the first full-scale historical account of the rise and growth of the jury system in England. The American edition adds a number of notes, as well as making several corrections to American references.

New York Field Codes. 1850-1865.
Vol. I. *The Code of Civil Procedure of the State of New-York, Reported Complete by the Commissioners on Practice and Pleadings.* 1850.
Vol. II. *The Code of Criminal Procedure of the State of New York,Reported Complete by the Commissioners on Practice and Pleadings.* 1850.
Vol. III. *The Civil Code of the State of New York, Reported Complete by the Commissioners of the Code.* 1865.
Vol. IV. *The Penal Code of the State of New York, Reported Complete by the Commissioners of the Code.* 1865.
Vol. V. *The Political Code of the State of New York.* 1860.
With a new introduction by Michael Weber. Five volume series. [8], xcvi, 791; liii, [1], 486; cxii, 776; lxiv, 406, clxvii; xlvii, 607 pp. Reprinted June 1998 by The Lawbook Exchange, Ltd. ISBN 1-886363-40-4 (set). Cloth. $495.
* These five volumes contain the complete texts of the law codes drafted for New York State by David Dudley Field and his colleagues uring the years 1847 to 1865.

They include Field's two procedural codes and three substantive codes. Field was perhaps the leading American proponent of codification. He served with both groups of commissioners and, more than any other individual, was responsible for the drafting of all the codes. He has been called "an inexhaustible one man codifying machine." Field's codes had great impact both in the United States and internationally and clearly are worthy of study today. This reprint is prefaced with a new introduction by Michael Weber.

Notes on the Science of Government and the Relations of the States to the United States. *Raleigh C. Minor.* x, 192 pp. 1913. Reprinted 1995 by The Lawbook Exchange, Ltd. ISBN 1-886363-09-9. Cloth. $40.
* Minor (1869-1923) was an author, publicist, and teacher of law at the University of Virginia, where his father was only the fourth to become professor of law. Minor continued his father's excellence in legal education and was a pioneer in private international law or the conflict of laws. In his *Notes*, Minor presents a thorough overview of both government in general and the relationship of states to the federal government. Anyone interested in the question of states' rights—a debate that remains ongoing—will find much of value in Minor's analysis of the legal status of the states and federal government under the Constitution. After developing the basic features of government, Minor elaborates upon the States Rights and Nationalistic schools of thought, drawing upon numerous Supreme Court cases and the writings of Story, de Tocqueville, Webster, Calhoun, Madison, and others.

Select Essays in Anglo-American Legal History. *By Maitland, Pollock, Holmes, Beale, Holdsworth and Others. Compiled and Edited by a Committee of the Association of*

American Law Schools. Boston: Little, Brown, and Company, 1907. Three volumes. 847; 823; 862 pp. Reprinted 1992 by The Lawbook Exchange, Ltd. LC 91-77977. ISBN 0-9630106-0-1. Cloth. $195.
* Originally conceived as a companion volume to Pollock and Maitland's *History of English Law*, this valuable work of legal scholarship, long out-of-print, has become increasingly difficult to obtain. Its 76 essays fill some 2,500 pages. At the time of its original publication the *Harvard Law Review* stated: "No one can fail to be impressed with the deep research, the deliberate construction, and the substantial worth of these essays."

A Sketch of English Legal History. *Maitland, Frederick W., Montague, Francis S., Colby, James F.* New York: G.P. Putnam's Sons, 1915. x, 234pp. Reprinted August 1998 by The Lawbook Exchange, Ltd. LC 98-11337. ISBN 1-886363-50-1. Cloth. $50.

Slavery in the Courtroom. An Annotated Bibliography of American Cases. *Paul Finkelman.* Washington:Library of Congress, 1985. Illustrated. xxvii, 312pp. Reprinted April 1998 by The Lawbook Exchange, Ltd. LC 98-11284. ISBN 1-886363-48-X. Cloth. $85.
* *Slavery in the Courtroom* was first published in 1985 and the following year received the Joseph A. Andrews Award from the American Association of Law Libraries. The book provides a detailed discussion and analysis of the pamphlet materials on the law of slavery published in the United States and Great Britain. *Slavery in the Courtroom* also provides readers with easy access to an understanding of most of the important American and British cases on slavery, including Somerset v. Stewart (Eng., 1772), The United States v. Amistad (U.S., 1841), and Dred Scott v. Sanford (U.S., 1857).

Paul Finkelman holds the John F. Seiberling Chair in Constitutional Law at University of Akron School of Law.

He is the author of more than ten books and over 75 scholarly articles. He has lectured on American law throughout the United States, as well as in Europe and in South America.

The Struggle for Law. *Rudolph von Jhering. Translated from the Fifth German Edition by John J. Lalor. Second Edition, with an Introduction by Albert Kocourek* Chicago: Callaghan and Company, 1915. lii, 138 pp. Reprinted 1997 by The Lawbook Exchange, Ltd. ISBN 1-886363-25-0. Cloth. $60.

* Reprint of the second English edition (1915). First published in German in 1872 as *Der Kampf ums Recht*, the work attracted wide attention and was reissued in several revised editions and translated into a dozen foreign languages. The author was a renowned scholar of Roman law who wrote in a lively style. One legal historian called him "the Mark Twain of German jurisprudence." In this essay he discussed what the law is and how the law changes. It is a classic in the perennial struggle to make the law a means for achieving social change.

A Theory of the Common Law. *James Walker.* Boston: Little, Brown and Co., 1852. xxiv, 130pp. Reprinted September 1998 by The Lawbook Exchange, Ltd. LC 98-9522. ISBN 1-886363-45-5. Cloth. $65.

* Uncommon first and only edition of an original essay written by a successful lawyer and accomplished scholar from South Carolina. Untypical of most American practitioners at this time, Walker had a deep interest in Roman law, which is reflected here in numerous comparative references and in an earlier book by Walker on Roman law. Walker (1813-1854) was a graduate of the University of South Carolina and a member of the South Carolina bar; at the time of his premature death, he had already published three books. See Appleton's Cyclopaedia.1852.

Trust Estates as Business Companies. [Second Edition]. *John H. Sears.* Kansas City, Mo.:Vernon Law Book Company, 1921. xx, 782 pp. [1921]. Reprinted June 1998 by The Lawbook Exchange, Ltd. LC 97-32423 ISBN 1-886363-41-2. Cloth. New. $95.
* Sears invented the term "trust estates as business companies" which was recognized and defined in *Rawle's Third Revision of Bouvier's Law Dictionary.* A practical description of the law of trusts including historical perspectives into the origin of the modern "Massachusetts Business trust," arguably the only common-law method of business organization available with limited liability for the organizers, including the Standard Oil Trust. The text also includes a discussion of income taxation which is still of continued relevance in today's tax law, discussions of "Common Law Companies," "Business Trusts" and "Voluntary Associations" and relevant Massachusetts and Oklahoma statutes. The second edition is a significant update to the original 1912 edition.

The World's Most Famous Court Trial. Tennessee Evolution Case. *A Complete Stenographic Report of the Famous Court Test of the Anti-Evolution Act, at Dayton July 10 to 21, 1925, Including Speeches and Arguments of Attorneys.* Cincinnati: National Book Company,[1925]. [4], 339 pp. Reprinted 1997 by The Lawbook Exchange, Ltd. LC 97-38485. ISBN 1-886363-31-5. Cloth. $65.
* Complete transcript of the celebrated "monkey trial," the case of the State of Tennessee vs. John Thomas Scopes, a 24-year old high school teacher accused of violating a recently enacted state law that banned the teaching of Charles Darwin's theory of evolution. Perhaps the first modern "media event," the trial attracted enormous national and international attention. A star-studded cast of trial attorneys included the great orator

and three time Democratic presidential candidate William Jennings Bryan and the brilliant trial lawyer and champion of the downtrodden, Clarence Darrow, among others. The climax of the trial came on the seventh day when the defense put the senior Bryan on the stand as an expert on the Bible and he was ruthlessly interrogated by Darrow. As a milestone in the American struggle between modernity and the forces of Protestant fundamentalism, and a vivid manifestation of the clash between two valid principles—academic freedom and democratic control of the public schools—the Scopes case has tremendous historical significance. This edition also includes statements by scientists entered at the defense's request, and the text of a lengthy concluding speech that Bryan prepared but never delivered.

Legal Dictionaries

A Dictionary of Law. Containing Definitions of the Terms and Phrases of American and English Jurisprudence, Ancient and Modern. Including the Principal Terms of International, Constitutional, and Commercial Law; with a Collection of Legal Maxim and Numerous Select Titles from the Civil Law and Other Foreign Systems. [First edition]. *Henry Campbell Black.* St. Paul, Minn.: West Publishing, 1891. x, 1253 pp. Reprinted 1991 by the Lawbook Exchange, Ltd. ISBN 1-886363-10-2. Cloth. $125.

* Reprint of the rare first edition of the classic American Law Dictionary, now in its sixth edition. Contains definitions of the terms and phrases of American and English jurisprudence, ancient and modern (including the principal terms of international, constitutional, and commercial law). There is also a collection of legal maxims, as well as a bibliography of the principal law dictionaries in English and other languages to 1891.

A Law Dictionary. Containing Definitions of the Terms and Phrases of American and English Jurisprudence, Ancient and Modern. And Including the Principal Terms of International, Constitutional, Ecclesiastical and Commercial Law, and Medical Jurisprudence, with a Collection of Legal Maxims, Numerous Select Titles from the Roman, Modern Civil, Scotch, French, Spanish, and Mexican Law, and Other Foreign Systems, and a Table of Abbreviations. [Second Edition]. *Henry Campbell Black.* St. Paul, Minn.: West Publishing, 1910. 1314 pp. Reprinted 1995 by the Lawbook Exchange, Ltd. ISBN 1-886363-10-2. Cloth. $125.

* The second edition of Black's classic dictionary incorporates many new definitions and additional citations to decided cases, besides being a thorough revision of previous entries. Also included are many Latin and French terms overlooked in the first edition. Medical jurisprudence in particular is enriched, with new definitions for insanity and pathological and criminal insanity. The second edition (1910) is an essential complement to the first edition (1891) as it provides the scholar and student of law important insights into the rapid development of law at the turn of the century. The second edition is also notable for its revamped system of arrangement, with all compound and descriptive terms subsumed under their related main entries. Libraries, students, historians, and practitioners will all benefit from this historically significant research tool.

A Law Dictionary, Adapted to the Constitution and Laws of the United States of America, and of the Several States of the American Union; with References to the Civil and Other Systems of Foreign Law. [First edition]. *John Bouvier*. Philadelphia: T. & J.W.

Johnson, 1839. Two volumes. 559; 628 pp. Reprinted 1993 by the Lawbook Exchange, Ltd. ISBN 0-9630106-7-0. Cloth. $130.
* First American law dictionary to be published. Long recognized as a leading authority, all other American law dictionaries are inevitably compared with this one. A concise encyclopedia of Anglo-American law, its outstanding feature is its emphasis on the American elements in the law. The original volumes are quite rare.

A Dictionary of American and English Law with Definitions of the Technical terms of the Canon and Civil Laws. Also, Containing a Full Collection of Latin Maxims, and Citations of Upwards of Forty Thousand Reported Cases, in which Words and Phrases Have Been Judicially Defined or Construed. *Stewart Rapalje and Robert L. Lawrence.* Jersey City: Frederick C. Linn & Co., 1888. Two volumes. xxxviii, 1380 pp. Reprinted 1997 by The Lawbook Exchange, Ltd. LC 97-38484. ISBN 1-886363-33-1. Cloth. $195.
* Rapalje was the author of criminal law treatises and compiled digests, having worked with Benjamin Vaughan Abbott to create the problematic *United States Digest New Series*. He was said to have learned from "the faults of his tutor" and this work has been cited for its correctness and usefulness.

A Dictionary of Law, Consisting of Judicial Definitions and Explanations of Words, Phrases, and Maxims, and an Exposition of the Principles of Law: Comprising a Dictionary and Compendium of American and English Jurisprudence. *William C. Anderson.* Chicago: T.H. Flood and Company, 1889. viii, 1140pp. Reprinted 1996 by The Lawbook Exchange, Ltd. ISBN 1-886363-23-4. Cloth. $125.
* A significant early American law dictionary that preceded Black's by two years. Black in fact

acknowledged his debt to Anderson in the preface of his first edition, and a comparison of entries reveals many instances of similar if not identical language, though both lexicographers have drawn freely from previous works. Anderson's *Dictionary* is heavily referenced, citing countless cases, treatises and other sources. Moreover, many entries, such as citizen and law itself, receive extended treatment. Anderson gives judicially framed definitions whenever possible to illustrate the application of judicial principles. Preferred spellings and the correct pronunciation of often mispronounced words are included, as are Latin and Norman-French terms, and brief biographies of prominent jurists such as Blackstone, Kent, and Story. Anderson's *Dictionary* is an authoritative legal reference work for all libraries.

A New Law Dictionary and Glossary: Containing Full Definitions of the Principal Terms of the Common and Civil Law, Together with Translations and Explanations of the Various Technical Phrases in Different Languages, Occurring in the Ancient and Modern Reports, and Standard Treatises; Embracing Also All the Principal Common and Civil Law Maxims. Compiled on the Basis of Spelman's Glossary, and Adapted to the Jurisprudence of the United States; with Copious Illustrations, Critical and Historical. *Alexander M. Burrill.* Critical and Historical. New York: John S. Voorhies, 1850. Two volumes. xviii, 1099 pp. Reprinted 1998 by The Lawbook Exchange, Ltd. LC 97-38481. ISBN 1-886363-32-3. Cloth. $175.

* First edition. A scarce, important original American dictionary by a student of James Kent. Burrill (1807-1869) was admitted to the New York Bar in 1828. Among his peers, Burrill was highly regarded for his legal scholarship.

Dictionary of American Biography describes this as "a work of very high standard, which at once took its place as perhaps the best book of its kind so far produced... All his books were distinguished for their graceful style and a scholarly precision and finish which earned the unstinted commendation of the judiciary. In addition their accuracy of statement and definition was fully recognized at the time by the profession at large."

Tayler's Law Glossary. Being a Selection of the Greek, Latin, Saxon, French, Norman and Italian Sentences, Phrases, and Maxims, Found in the Leading English and American Reports, and Elementary Works. [Fourth Edition]. *Thomas Tayler*. New York: Lewis & Blood, 1856. 580 pp. Reprinted 1995 by The Lawbook Exchange, Ltd. ISBN 1-886363-12-9. Cloth. $65.
* This early dictionary offers a unique historical perspective on the state of American law in the mid-eighteenth century. It contains translations of nearly five-thousand items of foreign origin and supplies definitions for innumerable maxims of law found in both English and American sources. The author has paid great attention to the context of legal terms and supplies extensive notes, with citations, after each section of his glossary (i.e., after "A", "B", "C", etc.). This glossary is an important research tool that will aid greatly in elucidating both the source and meaning of legal concepts of the last century.

Legal Bibliography & Reference

Acts and Laws of the Thirteen Original Colonies and States: Constituting the extraordinary collection of Hon. Russell Benedict. New York. 1922. [252pp]. Reprinted August 1998 by The Lawbook Exchange, Ltd. LC 98-20196 ISBN 1-886363-56-0. Cloth. $85.

Anglo-American Legal Bibliographies. An Annotated Guide. *William L. Friend.* Washington, D.C.: United States Government Printing Office, 1944. Illustrated. xii, 166 pp. Reprinted 1996 by The Lawbook Exchange, Ltd. ISBN 1-886363-21-8. Cloth. $65.

* This extensively annotated bibliography provides a complete bibliographical analysis of 298 significant works in Anglo-American legal literature. Friend has omitted "nothing of legal bibliographical importance" in his descriptions and has included the Library of Congress catalogue entry and number for each title. Entries are arranged in alphabetical order by author, followed by a comprehensive index. Friend introduces his study with a lengthy historical survey of the important developments in legal bibliography.

Bibliotheca Legum Angliae. Or, a Catalogue of the Common and Statute Law Books of This Realm, and Some Others Relating Thereto: Giving an Account of Their Several Editions, Ancient Printers, Dates, and Prices, and Wherein They Differ. [With a Supplement to 1800]. *Part I Compiled by John Worrall, Part II and Supplement Compiled by Edward Brooke.* Parts I, II and Supplement bound in one volume. II and Supplement bound in one volume. London: Printed for Edward Brooke, 1788-1800. 316; 264; 48 pp. Reprinted 1997 by The Lawbook Exchange, Ltd. ISBN 1-886363-29-3. Cloth. $110.

* First annotated English legal bibliography. John Worrall, believed to be the first law bookseller, issued the first edition in 1732. He published numerous editions during his lifetime. After Worrall's death in 1771 it was continued by Edward Brooke and later John Clarke. This edition of the important early bibliography consists of a reprint of Parts I and II of the 1788 edition, and includes the uncommon supplement to 1800. In this edition Part I

continued Worrall's work with the addition of many titles, a wider range of subject headings, and extension of the experiment begun in the 1782 edition of including observations by learned law writers in the annotation to some entries. This last development marked a positive step of the bare Bassett style of catalogue, which Worrall had originally followed and which was to influence future bibliographies. Part II provides a historical account of English legal literature from the earliest times to the reign of George III.

A Complete List of British and Colonial Law Reports and Legal Periodicals. Arranged in Alphabetical and in Chronological Order with Bibliographical Notes. With a Check List of Canadian Statutes. [Third Edition]. *W. Harold Maxwell and C.R. Brown.* Toronto: The Carswell Company, Limited, 1937. viii, 141, 49 pp. Reprinted 1995 by The Lawbook Exchange, Ltd. ISBN 1-886363-11-0. Cloth. $70.

* This comprehensive guide includes every known edition of every British or Colonial law report (except American reprints). This edition also includes a list of the various territories in the British Empire which had issued printed legislation. Librarians and scholars will find this a particularly useful checklist, with notes that supplement Soule's earlier *Lawyer's Reference Manual.*

Latin for Lawyers. With 1000 Legal Maxims. *E. Hilton Jackson.* London: Sweet & Maxwell, 1915. viii, 300 pp. Reprinted 1992 by The Lawbook Exchange, Ltd. LC 92-074408. ISBN 0-9630106-4-6. Cloth. $50.

* The perfect book for that considerable number of law students and lawyers with little or no knowledge of Latin. For those already proficient in Latin, the interest in this volume will lie in the large collection of legal maxims and phrases. The annotations are commendable for their brevity and unpretentious simplicity.

Men and Books Famous in the Law. *Frederick C. Hicks. With an introduction by Harlan F. Stone.* Rochester, New York: Lawyers Co-operative Publishing, 1921. 259 pp. Reprinted 1992 by The Lawbook Exchange, Ltd. LC 92-070809. ISBN 0-9630106-2-X. Cloth. $50.
* A classic account of law books and their authors. Within the pages of this volume will be found the stories of great legal writers, and more especially the story of their legal writings, the inception, production, and vicissitudes of works which have become classics of legal literature. Covers the lives and publications of Littleton, Coke, Blackstone, Cowell, Kent, Wheaton and Livingston.

Ragbag of Legal Quotations. *Compiled by M. Frances McNamara.* Albany: Matthew Bender & Company, 1960. xi, 334 pp. Reprinted 1992 by The Lawbook Exchange, Ltd. LC 92-074141. ISBN 0-9630106-3-8. Cloth. $50.
* One of the best collections of legal quotations ever. McNamara's attractive and well-indexed volume provides over 2,000 quotations arranged under nearly 300 subject headings, which are further indexed by author and by words and phrases. Explanatory notes clarify the meaning of some well-known, but misunderstood quotations.

The William Blackstone Collection in the Yale Law Library. A Bibliographical Catalogue. *Catherine Spicer Eller.* New Haven: Yale University Press, 1938. xvii,134 pp. Reprinted 1993 by The Lawbook Exchange, Ltd. ISBN 0-9630106-5-4. Cloth. $50.
The *William Blackstone Collection* bibliography is primarily a description of the *Blackstoniana* in the Yale Law Library and the Yale University Library, but with additional information concerning editions not held by Yale. It is believed to describe the most comprehensive collection of editions and abridgments of the *Commentaries* to be

found in any one library. Friend, *Anglo-American Legal Bibliographies*, p. 69. Includes not only the *Commentaries*, but all legal works of William Blackstone, as well as pertinent criticism.

❧*Law & Literature*☙

Charles Dickens As a Legal Historian. *William S. Holdsworth.* New Haven: Yale University Press, 1929. 157 pp. Reprinted 1995 by The Lawbook Exchange, Ltd. ISBN 1-886363-06-4. Cloth. $40.

* The distinguished English historian, Professor Holdsworth, has contrived even during his moments of recreation to render us his debtors. No two books outside the bounds of technical law are more worth reading for law students than *Pickwick Papers* and *Bleak House*. Even a trained trial lawyer however, is puzzled by some of the legal points brought up by Dickens, because they have fortunately passed forever out of the realm of living law. Professor Holdsworth has performed a valuable service to lawyers and laymen alike in explaining these obscurities. And he has done much more than this. He has increased our admiration for the genius of Dickens by proving his great merit as a legal historian. Zechariah Chafee, Jr. *Harvard Law Review* 42:286-8.

An Eye for an Eye. *Clarence S. Darrow.* 1905. New York: Fox Duffield & Company, 1905. 213 pp. Reprinted 1996 by The Lawbook Exchange, Ltd. ISBN 1-886363-07-2. Cloth. $40.

* *An Eye for an Eye* was Darrow's only fictional work, aside from his autobiographical novel, *Farmington*, published in 1904.It tells the story of Jim Jackson, who struggles with poverty and harsh circumstances, before finally murdering his wife in a fit of rage. Faced with the gallows, Jackson confesses: "If ther'd been forty scaffolds

right before my eyes, I'd have brought down the poker just the same." Darrow's novel is a sociological polemic which foreshadows such later works as Theodore Dreiser's *An American Tragedy* and Upton Sinclair's *The Jungle*. Abe Ravitz in his *Clarence Darrow and the American Literary Tradition* (1962), observed that *An Eye for an Eye* was worthy of a trophy not only for sociological veracity but also for genuine literary achievement.

A Persian Pearl. And Other Essays. *Clarence S. Darrow.* East Aurora, NY: The Roycroft Shop, 1899. 175 pp. Reprinted 1997 by The Lawbook Exchange, Ltd. ISBN 1-886363-27-7. Cloth. $50.

* Reprint of the first edition (1899) which was printed by Elbert Hubbard at the Roycroft Shop in an edition of 980 copies. Darrow's first book is rare and the cornerstone of any Darrow collection. It was preceded by only a few newspaper and periodical contributions and by two or three pamphlets. It consists of five essays, the title essay treating the *Rubaiyat of Omar Khayam*, with others on philosophical matters, Walt Whitman, realism in art and literature, and Robert Burns.

ꕥ *U.S. Constitutional History* ꕥ

Blackstone's Commentaries. With Notes of Reference to the Constitution and Laws, of the Federal Government of the United States, and of the Commonwealth of Virginia. In Five Volumes. With an Appendix to Each Volume, Containing Short Tracts upon Such Subjects As Appeared Necessary to Form a Connected View of the Laws of Virginia As a Member of the Federal Union. *St. George Tucker. With an introduction by Paul Finkelman and David Cobin.* Philadelphia: William Young Birch and Abraham Small, 1803. Five volumes. Reprinted 1996 by The Lawbook

Exchange, Ltd. ISBN 1-886363-15-3. Cloth. $450.
* The first extended treatment of the subject, *Tucker's Blackstone* is a key resource for understanding how Americans viewed English common law in the years following the adoption of the Constitution and the Bill of Rights. Based on his lectures at the College of William and Mary, Tucker interprets Blackstone's often antidemocratic viewpoint in the American context. A strong proponent of the First Amendment, he elaborates a theory of freedom of speech and press that is more expansive than in the English tradition. *Tucker's Blackstone* has been cited in numerous cases by the U.S. Supreme Court in an attempt to discern the "original intent" of the Constitution. A monumental work of continuing relevance, this reprint edition is prefaced by a new critical introduction by Professors Paul Finkelman and David Cobin.

A Brief Enquiry Into the True Nature and Character of Our Federal Government, being a review of Judge Story's Commentaries on the Constitution of the United States. By a Virginian. *[Upshur, Abel Parker].* Petersburg: Printed by Edmund and Julian C. Ruffin, 1840. 132pp. Reprinted May 1998 by The Lawbook Exchange, Ltd. LC 97-11151. ISBN 1-886363-44-7. Cloth. $45.
* A refutation of the nationalistic theory of the Constitution, originally published as a pamphlet in 1840, this work was also reprinted in 1863 by Northern Democrats in an effort to set forth the political philosophy of the Confederacy. Upshur (1791-1844), a Virginia judge, politician and spokesman for states-rights, proslavery southern conservative ideology, served as Secretary of the Navy and Secretary of State under President Tyler. An advocate of the annexation of Texas and reopened those negotations. He was a supporter of

banking regulation and an opponent of the theory of natural law. The original edition, published by another Southern conservative, Edmund Ruffin, is now quite uncommon.

Citizenship Sovereignty. *John S. Wright.* Chicago: Published for American Citizens, the True Maintainers of State Sovereignty, 1864. 12, [1], viii, 208, [2] pp. Reprinted September 1998 by The Lawbook Exchange, Ltd. LC 98-15940. ISBN 1-886363-55-2. Cloth. $65.
* Reprint of the scarce first edition. Defines and examines the concept of citizenship and its relation to the sovereignty of this nation and of states. Wright built the first public school building erected in Chicago, and was a strong and consistent supporter of public education. Chicago Pre-Fire Imprints 764.

Commentaries on the Laws of Virginia. Comprising the Substance of a Course of Lectures Delivered to the Winchester Law School. *Henry St. George Tucker. With an Introduction by David Cobin and Paul Finkelman.* Richmond: Shepherd and Colin, 1846. Two volumes. 34, 468; 24, 512 pp. Reprinted May 1998 by The Lawbook Exchange, Ltd. LC 97-10313. ISBN 1-886363-26-9. Cloth. $175.
* Along with James Kent's Commentaries on American Law, and Joseph Story's Commentaries, Tucker's two volume work established the standard for American treatise writing, and helped organize American law. The *Commentaries* served as the primary reference source for the bar of Virginia as well as for many in the rest of the country until 1850, and was considered the most valuable text for students and lawyers in much of the South until the Civil War.

While modeled on Blackstone's *Commentaries*, Tucker's work is entirely original. In that way it is a much more impressive accomplishment than his father's edition of

Blackstone. The senior Tucker labored hard to annotate Blackstone, and then add to it; Henry wrote his *Commentaries on the Laws of Virginia* himself, based on his lectures at Winchester Law School, which he established in 1824. *The Commentaries on the Laws of Virginia* cover in detail the subject matter in the first three Blackstone's *Commentaries*.

Construction Construed and Constitutions Vindicated. *John Taylor.* Richmond: printed by Shepherd & Pollard, 1820. iv, 344pp. Reprinted August 1998 by The Lawbook Exchange, Ltd. LC 97-49411. ISBN 1-886363-43-9. Cloth. $65.

* One of the major works of the Virginian John Taylor of Caroline (1753-1824). Little-known today, Taylor's work is of great significance in the political and intellectual history of the South and is essential for understanding the constitutional theories that Southerners asserted to justify secession in 1861.

Taylor fought in the Continental army during the American Revolution and served briefly in the Virginia House of Delegates and as a U.S. Senator. It was as a writer on constitutional, political, and agricultural questions, however, that Taylor gained prominence. He joined with Thomas Jefferson and other agrarian advocates of states' rights and a strict construction of the Constitution in the political battles of the 1790s. His first published writings argued against Secretary of the Treasury Alexander Hamilton's financial program.

Construction Construed and Constitutions Vindicated was Taylor's response to a series of post-War of 1812 developments including John Marshall's Supreme Court decision in McCulloch v. Maryland, the widespread issuance of paper money by banks, proposals for a protective tariff, and the attempt to bar slavery from Missouri. Along with many other Southerners, Taylor feared that these and other measures following in the train of Hamilton's financial system, were undermining the foundations of American republicanism. He saw them as the attempt of an "artificial capitalist sect" to corrupt the virtue of the American people and upset the proper consitutional balance between state and federal authority in favor of a centralized national government. Taylor wrote, "If the means to which the government of the union may resort for executing the power confided to it, are unlimited, it may easily select such as will impair or destroy the powers confided to the state governments."

Jefferson, who noted that "Col. Taylor and myself have rarely, if ever, differed in any political principle of importance," considered *Construction Construed and Constitutions Vindicated* "the most logical retraction of our governments of our governments to the original and true principles of the Constitution creating them, which has appeared since the adoption of the instrument." Later Southern thinkers, notably John C. Calhoun, were clearly indebted to Taylor.

The Evolution of the Constitution of the United States. Showing That It Is a Development of Progressive History and Not an Isolated Document Struck Off at a Given Time or an Imitation of English or Dutch Forms of Government. *Sydney George Fisher.* Philadelphia: J.B. Lippincott Company, 1897. 398 pp. Reprinted 1996 by The Lawbook Exchange, Ltd. LC 97-41054. ISBN 1-886363-08-0. Cloth. $65.

* Fisher (1856-1927) was a prominent historian and lawyer, who was admitted to the Pennsylvania bar in 1883 after legal studies at Harvard University. His *Evolution of the Constitution* collates for the first time all the various provisions of colonial documents that served as source material for the Constitution. Asserting that the Constitution was neither an imitation nor an invention,

Fisher traces every material clause back to its origin. Twenty-nine colonial charters and constitutions, seventeen Revolutionary constitutions, and twenty-three plans of union are the resulting source materials from which Fisher draws his analysis. Abundant quotations from the sixty-nine documents illustrate the evolutionary nature of the Constitution and make this a valuable sourcebook for the reader who desires to find in one volume the Constitution's many and varied origins.

An Inquiry into the Principles and Policy of the Government of the United States. *John Taylor.* Fredericksburg:Green and Cady, 1814. With an introduction by Roy Franklin Nichols, Yale University Press, 1950. 562pp. Reprinted May 1998 by The Lawbook Exchange, Ltd. LC 98-11147. ISBN 1-886363-46-3.Cloth. $75.

* Considered a political writing that "deserves to rank among the two or three really historic contributions to political science which have been produced in the United States" (Beard, *Economic Origins of Jeffersonian Democracy*), this work was originally conceived in 1794 as a response to John Adams' *A Defence of the Constitutions of Government of the United States of America* and first published in 1814. He rejects the concept of "a natural aristocracy" of "paper and patronage" and a federal government based on a system of debt and taxes. Opposed to the extent of power awarded to the executive office, he calls for a shortening of the terms of the president and all elected officers. He considers the American government to be one of divided powers rather than classes, and its agents responsible to sovereign people alone.

Taylor (1808-1887) was known as "John Taylor of Caroline County, Virginia" and served in the Continental Army and later in the Virginia House of Delegates, then served three separate terms as member of the United

States Senate. He is considered to be one of the nation's greatest philosophers of agrarian liberalism, and wrote extensively on this topic as well as on political matters. One of the nation's first proponents of states rights, in 1798 he introduced into the Virginia legislature resolutions in support of the doctrine of delegated powers.

A Treatise on the Constitutional Limits Which Rest Upon the Legal Power of The United States of the American Union. Fifth edition. *Thomas E. Cooley.* Boston: Little, Brown, and Co., 1883. lxxxi, 886pp. Reprinted August 1998 by The Lawbook Exchange, Ltd. LC 98-12730. ISBN 1-886363-53-6. Cloth. $120.

Twice Condemned: Slaves and the Criminal Laws of Virginia, 1705-1865. *Philip J. Schwarz.* [Baton Rouge: Louisiana State University Press]. [1988]. xvi, 354pp. Reprinted May 1998 The Lawbook Exchange, Ltd. LC 98-4424 ISBN 1-886363-54-4. Cloth. $75.

* Analyzes the history of enslaved African Americans' relationship with the criminal courts of the Old Dominion during a 160 year period. Before *Twice Condemned* was first published in 1988, historians often focused primarily on isolated or dramatic examples of the sometimes deadly conflict present in societies based on slave labor. But *Twice Condemned* analyzes the prevalance, longevity, and variety of behavior attributed to slave convicts. In doing so, this book also provides a detailed picture of how one slave society evolved, of some previously unexamined aspects of slave culture, and of slaveowners' attitudes toward the "domestic enemy" in their midst.

Schwarz' study is based on over four thousand trials from the colonial, early national, and antebellum periods. *Twice Condemned* traces the manner in which slaves' and whites' conflicting perceptions of legitimate behavior informed their actions. The judicial system for slaves served two purposes: it helped slaveowners control slaves and enabled authorities to sanction criminal behavior. This dual function of slave trials mirrored the two kinds of slaves' behavior judges tried to suppress. Slaves' overt resistance to bondage was regularly curtailed and antisocial and dangerous actions were sometimes punished.

Twice Condemned provides a fascinating portrayal of slave culture and slave resistance to white society not only as a means of resistance against oppression but as a means of individual empowerment.

ꕥ *Special Editions* ꕥ

The Iconography of Manhattan Island 1498-1909. *I.N. Phelps Stokes.* New York: Robert H. Dodd,1915. Six volumes. Reprinted July 1998 by The Lawbook Exchange, Ltd. LC 97-30604. ISBN 1-886363-30-7. Cloth. $750.

* Reprint edition of Stokes' magnificent and comprehensive illustrated history of Manhattan. This sweeping survey, originally published over the span 1915 to 1928, is divided into two parts, with volumes one and two comprising the first. These initial volumes present historical summaries, followed by exquisite plates and thorough plate descriptions. Part two repeats this pattern in volume three; presents a detailed chronology of historical events and personages in volumes four and five; and concludes with an addenda, bibliography, and index to the entire work in volume six. Interspersed throughout are the maps, documents, photographs, engravings, illustrations, etc. that Stokes and his assistants assembled from countless original sources. The quality and scope of visual representations truly befits its vast subject, Manhattan.